Real-Life Decision-Making

Have you ever experienced a decision situation that was hard to come to grips with? Did you ever feel a need to improve your decision-making skills? Is this something where you feel that you have not learned enough practical and useful methods? In that case, you are not alone! Even though decision-making is both considered and actually is a very important skill in modern work-life as well as in private life, these skills are not to any reasonable extent taught in schools at any level. No wonder many people do indeed feel the need to improve but have a hard time finding out how. This book is an attempt to remedy this shortcoming of our educational systems and possibly also of our common, partly intuition-based, decision culture. Intuition is not at all bad, quite the contrary, but it has to co-exist with rationality. We will show you how.

Methods for decision-making should be of prime concern to any individual or organisation, even if the decision processes are not always explicitly or even consciously formulated. All kinds of organisations, as well as individuals, must continuously make decisions of the most varied nature in order to prosper and attain their objectives. A large part of the time spent in any organisation, not least at management levels, is spent gathering, processing, and compiling information for the purpose of making decisions supported by that information. The same interest has hitherto not been shown for individual decision-making, even though large gains would also be obtained at a personal level if important personal decisions were better deliberated. This book aims at changing that and thus attends to both categories of decision-makers.

This book will take you through a journey starting with some history of decision-making and analysis and then go through easy-to-learn ways of structuring decision information and methods for analysing the decision situations, beginning with simple decision situations and then moving on to progressively harder ones, but never losing sight of the overarching goal that the reader should be able to follow the progression and being able to carry out similar decision analyses in real-life situations.

Real-Life Decision-Making

Mats Danielson and Love Ekenberg

CRC Press
Taylor & Francis Group
Boca Raton London New York

CRC Press is an imprint of the
Taylor & Francis Group, an **informa** business

Designed cover image: Shutterstock

First edition published 2024
by CRC Press
6000 Broken Sound Parkway NW, Suite 300, Boca Raton, FL 33487-2742

and by CRC Press
4 Park Square, Milton Park, Abingdon, Oxon, OX14 4RN

Library of Congress Cataloging-in-Publication Data

Names: Danielson, Mats (Professor of computer and systems sciences),
author. | Ekenberg, Love, author.
Title: Real-life decision-making / Mats Danielson and Love Ekenberg.
Description: 1 Edition. | Boca Raton : CRC Press, 2024. | Includes
bibliographical references and index.
Identifiers: LCCN 2023011479 (print) | LCCN 2023011480 (ebook) |
ISBN 9781032524382 (hardback) | ISBN 9781032524399 (paperback) |
ISBN 9781003406709 (ebook)
Subjects: LCSH: Decision making. | Practical reason. | Leadership.
Classification: LCC HD69.C6 D346 2024 (print) | LCC HD69.C6 (ebook) |
DDC 658.4/03--dc23/eng/20230313
LC record available at https://lccn.loc.gov/2023011479
LC ebook record available at https://lccn.loc.gov/2023011480

ISBN: 9781032524382 (hbk)
ISBN: 9781032524399 (pbk)
ISBN: 9781003406709 (ebk)

DOI: 10.1201/9781003406709

Typeset in Adobe Caslon Pro
by KnowledgeWorks Global Ltd.

This book is dedicated to the co-author, dear friend, and esteemed colleague Professor Love Ekenberg, who passed away in September 2022 during the writing of this book.

Contents

PREFACE   ix
ABOUT THE AUTHORS   xiii

CHAPTER 1   INTRODUCTION   1
            1.1   A Brief History of Decision Theory   2
            1.2   The Origin of Decision Analysis   6

CHAPTER 2   DECISION MODELLING   11
            2.1   Decisions under Certainty   14
            2.2   Decisions under Strict Uncertainty   14

CHAPTER 3   BAYESIAN DECISION ANALYSIS   21

CHAPTER 4   IMPRECISE INFORMATION   35
            4.1   Imprecise Probability   36
            4.2   A Decision Process   40
            4.3   A Decision Example   45

CHAPTER 5   MULTI-CRITERIA DECISION-MAKING   53
            5.1   Proportional Scoring   55
            5.2   Ratio Scoring   57
            5.3   Ranking   57
            5.4   Other Approaches   58
            5.5   Rank Three   59

CHAPTER 6 THE PILOT METHOD   63
           6.1 Stage 1 – P-C Lists   65
           6.2 Finishing after Stage 1   67
           6.3 Stage 2 – An Argument Matrix   68
           6.4 Finishing after Stage 2   70
           6.5 Stage 3 – Ranking the Alternatives   71
           6.6 Finishing after Stage 3   74
           6.7 Stage 4 – Ranking the Criteria   75
           6.8 Finishing after Stage 4   78
           6.9 Stage 5 – Separate Cost Analysis   79
           6.10 Summary   83

CHAPTER 7 REAL-LIFE CASE STUDIES   85
           7.1 Procurement   85
           7.2 Policy Formation for Catastrophic Events 89
           7.3 Energy Planning   93

CHAPTER 8 GUIDELINES FOR REAL-LIFE DECISIONS   99
           8.1 Single-Criterion Decisions   99
           8.2 Multi-Criteria Decisions   102

APPENDIX: THE DECIDEIT SOFTWARE   105
           A.1 Step 1 – Identify and Name the Criteria
                and the Alternatives   108
           A.2 Step 2 – Enter Information about the
                Strategies (Alternatives)   108
           A.3 Step 3 – Determine the Importance
                of the Criteria   110
           A.4 Step 4 – Evaluation   111
           A.5 Installation   114
           A.6 Licence Key Entry   115

READING TIPS   117

REFERENCES   119

INDEX   123

Preface

Have you ever experienced a decision situation that was hard to come to grips with? Did you ever feel a need to improve your decision-making skills? Is this something where you feel that you have not learned enough practical and useful methods? In that case, you are not alone! Even though decision-making is both considered and actually is a very important skill in modern work-life as well as in private life, these skills are not to any reasonable extent taught in schools at any level. No wonder many people do indeed feel the need to improve but have a hard time finding out how. This book is an attempt to remedy this shortcoming of our educational systems and possibly also of our common human, partly intuition-based, culture in general across the globe. Intuition is not at all bad, quite the contrary, but it has to co-exist with rationality. We will show you how.

Methods for decision-making should be of prime concern to any individual or organisation, even if the decision processes are not always explicitly or even consciously formulated. All kinds of organisations, as well as individuals, must continuously make decisions of the most varied nature in order to prosper and attain their objectives. A large part of the time spent in any organisation, not least at management levels, is spent gathering, processing, and compiling information for the purpose of making decisions supported by that information. The same interest has hitherto not been shown for individual decision-making, even though large gains would also be obtained at a personal level if important personal decisions were better deliberated. This book attends to both categories of decision-makers.

Real-life decision-making could, if taken seriously, include many components, such as trade-offs between different, sometimes conflicting, aspects of the situation, different value uncertainties as well as people with a variety of preferences. Some common features of such decision situations are that they might involve different stakeholders and opinions and can contain significant uncertainties due to a lack of full knowledge and interacting narratives as well as a risk for serious consequences depending on the choice of alternatives. In this book, we present decision methods for dealing with such situations that help us to choose a path also when we have incomplete knowledge. The basic idea is that we have different alternatives to deal with. These might entail consequences that could be considered from different perspectives. The consequences and/or the alternatives might be evaluated in a variety of ways under different criteria. It is seldom a matter of finding the ultimate option but rather of refining what can be refined so that the available information becomes as clear as possible and that one thereby can base the decision-making on a transparent foundation.

Following the success of mathematical methods for solving management problems during the Second World War, a number of models for decision analysis were proposed in the 1950s. Thus, decision methodology, mainly in the form of utility theory, decision theory, and decision analysis, has been studied for a fairly long time. Not least, a number of Nobel Prize winners in economics have worked in this area. These include Kenneth Arrow (1972), Herbert Simon (1978), Maurice Allais (1988), Daniel Kahneman (2002), and Leonid Hurwicz (2007). Most of them worked with normative theory, i.e. how we should rightfully act. However, the results are usually in an idealised and theorised form that cannot easily be applied directly in decision-making situations, neither in organisations, nor in everyday life. Normative research is therefore not such a great help to us when making real-life decisions of any reasonable quality. Normative theories say "this is the outcome if you are deciding in an optimal way" but say little about how to get there. They are about as useful in everyday life as theoretical descriptions of how to ride a bicycle. You cannot just read the descriptions and then peddle off.

Kahneman, however, belongs to a different genre, the descriptive one, which studies and describes what people really do when they make decisions. Not surprisingly, people underperform in many situations and their brains are fooled by all sorts of information and disinformation. This can be very amusing to read about, and we highly recommend Kahneman's successful book *Thinking, Fast and Slow* (2011) for both entertainment and thought-provoking reading. But what we really need in real life is perhaps not a catalogue of mistakes but rather a method that carries us in a reasonably clear and safe way from decision problems to actual decisions. Descriptive research, therefore, is unfortunately not of that much help to us either when we are going to make real-life decisions of good quality. Continuing the cycling analogy: reading about bicycle accidents and how riders fell off their bikes and how large their wounds were will not help us much either. We will still not be able to peddle off after reading about them.

Fortunately, there is a third research direction, the lesser known prescriptive one, which focuses on procedures for carrying out and analysing real-life decisions and which the authors of this book have worked with for over a quarter of a century. The prescriptive perspective can in one sense be seen as the golden mean between the normative and descriptive ones and draws on knowledge from both. But the prescriptive stance is actually quite much more than that, in its relentless ambition to teach you how to think and what to do in real-life decision situations. Good prescriptive methods are like X-ray devices – seeing through the complexities of decision situations and moving right to the core. Thus, the purpose of this book is to demonstrate the usefulness of systematic and transparent prescriptive decision methods for handling sometimes complex but always real-life decision situations.

Mats Danielson
Love Ekenberg
September 2022

About the Authors

Mats Danielson is a Full Professor in Computer and Systems Sciences at Stockholm University, a Senior Advisor to the President, and a UNESCO Chair Professor. He is a former Dean of the Faculty of Social Sciences as well as a former Vice President for External Relations, Innovation, and ICT. He has a PhD in Computer and Systems Sciences from KTH Royal Institute of Technology (KTH) as well as university degrees in Computer Science and Engineering (from KTH) and in Economics and Business Administration (from Stockholm University). He worked in the software industry for almost 20 years before joining academia to work with research and algorithm and software design and development within decision analysis and decision support.

Love Ekenberg was a Full Professor in Computer and Systems Sciences at Stockholm University and was a UNESCO Professor. He received a PhD in Computer and Systems Sciences as well as a PhD in Mathematics, both from Stockholm University. He worked with risk and decision analysis, i.e. with development of theoretical frameworks and models, products, and methodologies within these areas, for more than 20 years, along with carrying out a large number of consultancy assignments.

1

INTRODUCTION

We might assume that we are free to choose in some sense, but at the same time, we are obliged not to behave indiscriminately. Unfortunately, in real life, many decisions are influenced by emotional impulses coloured through preconceptions and sometimes even shortcomings – it is all too easy to fall back instinctively into ingrained patterns whether these are reasonable or not. When the mind is stressed or overworked, it goes back to some kind of habitual base reactions – if you usually run, you run; if you usually fight, you fight. This fight-or-flight response is well documented in several disciplines, not least psychology, and is deeply rooted in our brains in order for us to be able to act without conscious decision-making in time-wise critical situations. In modern society, however, there are two problems with this response. First, most decision situations do not call for such a swift response, making that decision method and response less useful. Second, we are often nowadays not able to respond by either fleeing or fighting back (in any reasonable sense). Thus, we are rather caught in fight-flight-fright situations, where fright stands for having to absorb the stress and fear in situations in which the prevalent decision stress can only be swallowed rather than acted upon. This is far too common today and leads to more and more pent-up decision stress within us unless we have useful mechanisms and procedures for making good decisions.

We propose that in order to be able to act in a reasonable way, we could be fruitfully aided by structured decision methods, both to increase the possibility of understanding our own actions and to be able to actually assess the situation before we make a decision. So what should methods for decision-making look like when we do not possess complete or absolute knowledge of how we should act? There are, of course, situations where the choice is self-evident, given the values embraced, but quite often we confront situations where even

DOI: 10.1201/9781003406709-1
1

a solid comprehension is not enough or situations whose context we ourselves may not fully understand. Thus, we need some kinds of decision methods that are based on reasonable principles and understandable guidelines.

If we attempt to try to figure out how to conceive such methods, we can see that in decision-making situations, there are usually different components such as actors, alternatives of action, and consequences of these actions. The consequences, which might be considered under different perspectives or criteria, are then evaluated in different ways, and further, they might occur with different probabilities. But given that we have some (limited) knowledge about these components, how should we act? We need some kind of decision rule. Informally, we can think of a decision rule as something you can use as a yardstick to make a decision. "Consistently take the top fruit in a fruit bowl" might be a (albeit limited and not always very wise) decision rule. Broadly speaking, there are two types of decision rules. Decision rules where only the consequences of an action are taken into account are called teleological rules. There are also so-called deontic rules, taking other properties into account such as the virtue of the decision-maker or the mode in which a decision is made. Deontic rules have been around since the dawn of humanity and teleological rules have a long history as well, the latter of which we will now shortly overview. Thus, before we go deeper into what actually constitutes modern decision theory and decision analysis, let us have a look at how we reached where we are now. A reader who is more interested in practical applications of real-life decision-making rather than its roots can skip the rest of this chapter, which is a bit harder to read, without loss of continuity or understanding.

1.1 A Brief History of Decision Theory

Cogito, ergo sum (I think, therefore I am). Following his own words, the French philosopher René Descartes concluded in 1637 the existence of free will without the presence of pre-determinism. In a non-deterministic world, we are capable of choosing for ourselves from the possible courses of action we identify. But with the right to choose comes the responsibility for the consequences of our actions. It is up to us to discriminate between the different alternatives, and we are expected to do the right thing. The majority of such discriminations are trifling little choices, natural parts of our everyday lives, but some are of larger importance so that a structured and well-deliberated approach would be desired and a careful analysis should be undertaken before choosing and following a particular course of action.

However, the origin of the field of decision theory can be traced back to long before Descartes' meditation. The theory has evolved from the statistical aspects of games. Fibonacci's *Liber Abaci* (1202) and Luca Paccioli's *Summa de arithmetica, geometria et proportionalità* (1494) constitute important early written works on the subject. Paccioli raises the question of how the stakes should be divided between two players of the ancient ball game of balla who have agreed to play until one of them won six rounds but were interrupted and could not continue when one player had won five rounds and his counterpart had won three. Later, Gerolamo Cardano (1501–1576) tried to answer the question in his *Liber de ludo aleae* (published posthumously in 1663), in which he formulated the fundamental concept of solving a probability problem by identifying a situation with equally likely outcomes. Pierre-Remond Montmort (1678–1719) furthered the early work on probability theory in his *Essay d' Analyse sur les Jeux de Hazard* (1708) where he wanted to show superstitious gamblers how to behave rationally.

Other important early contributors to a general theory of probability include Blaise Pascal (1623–1662) and Pierre de Fermat (1601–1665), who, after encountering a gambling question from the French nobleman Antoine Gombaud (a.k.a. Chevalier de Méré, 1607–1684), initiated an exchange of letters in which fundamental principles of probability theory were formulated. Gombaud's game consisted of throwing two six-sided dice 24 times, and the problem was to decide whether or not to bet even money on the occurrence of at least one pair of sixes among the 24 throws. A seemingly well-established but deceiving gambling rule had led Gombaud to believe that betting on a double-six in 24 throws would be profitable; however, his calculations had indicated the opposite.

The importance of statistics grew in the 17th and 18th centuries with the introduction of life annuities and insurance. Mortality statistics and annuities were research areas of Abraham de Moivre (1667–1754), and in his *Doctrine of Chances* (1718), he defines statistical independence between events. Later, in *Miscellanea Analytica* (1730), de Moivre introduced the, to this day, very influential normal distribution as an approximation of the binomial distribution for use in the prediction of gambles. In the second edition of *Miscellanea Analytica* (1738), de Moivre improved the formula for the normal distribution with the support of James Stirling (1692–1770).

Furthermore, Reverend Thomas Bayes (1702–1761), an English Presbyterian minister, famous for his posthumously published *An Essay Toward Solving a Problem in the Doctrine of Chances* in 1763, introduced the widely applied Bayes' theorem and the concept of Bayesian updating, i.e. how probabilities should be changed when new information arrives. As a result, Bayes is credited with the introduction of subjective probability theory as well as the theory of information, and parts of statistical reasoning are named after him. Bayes' conclusions were later accepted by Pierre-Simon Laplace (1749–1827) and published in his double volume *Théorie Analytique des Probabilités* in 1812. In this comprehensive work, Laplace investigated many fundamental concepts occurring in probability theory as well as methods of finding probabilities of compound events when the probabilities of their simple components are known.

Alongside the early development of a theory of probability, the Swiss physician and mathematician Daniel Bernoulli (1700–1782) wrote his landmark paper *Specimen Theoriae Novae de Mensura Sortis* in 1738, in which a motivation for the concept of utility is given, commonly referred to as his solution to the famous St. Petersburg Paradox posed in 1713 by Daniel Bernoulli's cousin, Nicolaus Bernoulli. The name St. Petersburg Paradox is due to the fact that the distinguished Bernoulli family was in many ways connected to the city of St. Petersburg. In this paradox, which is a thought experiment, Nicolaus Bernoulli considered a fair coin, defined by the property that the probability of a head is 1/2 (50%). This coin is tossed until a head appears. The gambler is rewarded with 2 ducats if the first head appears on the first trial, $2 \cdot 2$ ducats if the first head appears on the second trial, and so on. The expected monetary value of this game is $\frac{1}{2} \cdot 2 + \frac{1}{2} \cdot \frac{1}{2} \cdot 2 \cdot 2 + \frac{1}{2} \cdot \frac{1}{2} \cdot \frac{1}{2} \cdot 2 \cdot 2 \cdot 2 + \ldots = 1 + 1 + 1 + \ldots = \text{infinity}$. It is nevertheless very difficult to believe that any gambler would be willing to pay an infinite amount of money (or even close) to participate in such a game. Bernoulli, therefore, concluded that the expected monetary value of that game is inappropriate as a decision rule. Bernoulli's solution to this paradox involved two ideas that have had a great impact on decision theory as well as economic theory. First, he stated that the utility of money cannot be related to the amount of money in the same way as the sum grows; it rather grows at a decreasing rate.

> To make this clear it is perhaps advisable to consider the following example: Somehow a very poor fellow obtains a lottery ticket that will yield with equal probability either nothing or twenty thousand ducats. Will this man evaluate his chance of winning at ten thousand ducats? Would he not be ill-advised to sell this lottery ticket for nine thousand ducats? To me it seems that the answer is in the negative. On the other hand I am inclined to believe that a rich man would be ill-advised to refuse to buy the lottery ticket for nine thousand ducats. If I am not wrong then it seems clear that all men cannot use the same rule to evaluate the gamble […] the value of an item must not be based on its price, but rather on the utility it yields. The price of the item is dependent only on the thing itself and is equal for everyone; the utility, however, is dependent on the particular circumstances of the person making the estimate.

> **Bernoulli (1738, reprinted 1954)**

Bernoulli identified the value of the consequences of a choice as being different from the objective economical outcome, commonly referred to as the idea of diminishing marginal utility. Bernoulli's second idea was that a person's valuation of a risky prospect is not the expected return of that prospect but rather the prospect's expected utility, i.e. the sum of the possible outcomes' perceived respective utilities multiplied by their probabilities of occurring (which we will look closer into in Chapter 3). Thus, the expected utility is in a sense similar to the expected value but has taken subjective utility into account.

In the St. Petersburg Paradox, the value of the game is finite due to the principle of diminishing marginal utility. Originally, Bernoulli used a function dependent on the gambler's wealth prior to the gamble itself in order to arrive at a finite number. Subsequently, other functions have been suggested to the same effect. Consequently, people are only willing to pay a finite amount of money to participate, even though the expected monetary value of the game is indeed infinite.

1.2 The Origin of Decision Analysis

Decision analysis is often regarded as a conjunction of subjective probability and subjective utility where "subjective" indicates that these are estimates made by the decision-maker, most often because this is the only kind of information actually available at decision time. Frank Ramsey (1903–1930) suggested in 1926 a theory that integrated these two areas in his article *Truth and Probability*. In that article, he informally presented a general set of rules for comparisons between acts with uncertain outcomes. From this set of rules, he could justify a procedure to measure a person's degree of belief in different alternative courses of action.

Preceding Ramsey's work, the concept of degree of belief as an approach to subjective probability had been introduced by John Maynard Keynes (1883–1946) in his *A Treatise on Probability* from 1921. Subjective probability, as opposed to objective probability, means that the different values reflect the decision-maker's actual beliefs, thus they are a measure of the degree of belief in a statement. These beliefs are not necessarily logical or rational, and they should be interpreted in terms of the willingness to act in a certain way.

> [Under uncertainty] there is no scientific basis on which to form any calculable probability whatever. We simply do not know. Nevertheless, the necessity for action and for decision compels us as practical men to do our best to overlook this awkward fact and to behave exactly as we should if we had behind us a good Benthamite calculation of a series of prospective advantages and disadvantages, each multiplied by its appropriate probability waiting to be summed.
>
> **Keynes (1937)**

In contrast, an objective (or classic) view on probabilities says that probabilities are exogenously given by nature. In *Probability, Statistics and Truth* (1928), Richard von Mises (1883–1953) introduced the relative frequency view, which argues that the probability of a specific event in a particular trial is the relative frequency of occurrence of that event in an infinite sequence of similar trials.

The modern and formal approach to game theory is attributed to John von Neumann (1903–1957), who in *Zur Theorie der Gesellschaftsspiele* in 1928 laid the foundation for a theory of games and conflicting interests. Later he wrote, together with Oskar Morgenstern (1902–1976), the important book *Theory of Games and Economic Behaviour* that came out in 1944, in which they introduced a considerable number of important ideas such as the formalisation of utility theory per se and also a formalisation of the expected utility. These are deemed to be reasonable requisites for a rational decision-maker, and it is demonstrated that the decision-maker is obliged to prefer the strategy with the highest expected utility to act rationally, given that he or she acted in accordance with the rules. Of further importance, through this work, von Neumann and Morgenstern bridged the gap between the mathematics of rationality and the social sciences. However, von Neumann and Morgenstern did not take subjective (i.e. self-estimated) probability into account, rather they regarded probability in an objective sense. Thus, the decision-maker could not influence the probabilities. Leonard Savage (1917–1971) combined the ideas of Ramsey and those of von Neumann and Morgenstern in *The Theory of Statistical Decision* in 1951. Here, Savage gives a thorough treatment of a complete theory of subjective expected utility and associated utility functions.

In *Statistical Decision Functions* published in 1950, Abraham Wald (1902–1950) makes use of something called loss functions and an expected loss criterion, as opposed to utility functions and the expected utility criteria. Loss functions and expected loss criteria later become standard basic elements in what is commonly referred to as Bayesian or statistical decision theory (see Chapter 3). The term Bayesian derives from the fact that this theory utilises prior information and non-experimental sources of information. However, in the general case, it is easy to adjust Wald's statistical decision theory to include utilities even though Wald himself had an objective view of probabilities. His concern focused on characterising admissible acts and alternatives for experimentation, where an action is admissible if no other action is better. This can be seen as an early attempt to characterise decision rules, and we will discuss this in Chapter 2.

The use of formal methods and mathematics for evaluating possible alternatives had a considerable upswing during the Second World War, and following the war, the terms operations analysis and operations research became closely related to decision analysis. Later, the military branches of operational research were often studied together with topics such as management science, industrial engineering, and mathematical programming. Due to the well-foundedness of decision theory, research in artificial intelligence has merged classical theories of decision-making with other techniques for handling uncertainty into a subfield of artificial intelligence commonly referred to as uncertain reasoning.

In comparatively recent literature, many modern characterisations of decision theory and decision analysis are suggested. Three leading contemporary researchers, Simon French, Ralph Keeney, and Michael Resnik, respectively, have given their views on what constitutes the areas as follows:

Decision analysis is the term used to refer to the careful deliberation that precedes a decision. More particularly it refers to the quantitative aspects of that deliberation.

French (1988)

A philosophy, articulated by a set of logical axioms, and a methodology and collection of systematic procedures, based upon those axioms, for responsibly analyzing the complexities inherent in decision problems.

Keeney (1982)

Decision theory is the product of the joint efforts of economists, mathematicians, philosophers, social scientists, and statisticians toward making sense of how individuals and groups make or should make decisions.

Resnik (1987)

Decision theory serves different purposes. Throughout the 20th century, it has, for example, evolved into a widespread tool for economists, mainly for predicting how a population will react to changes in their environment. From this perspective, the logical foundation of the theory is less important, while rather the ability to predict the behaviour of decision-makers is what matters. When using decision theory in such contexts, the theory is said to be descriptive; thus, we speak in terms of descriptive decision theory. The aim of descriptive decision theory is to explain how decisions are being made and why human decision-makers choose to act in a certain way.

A central result is Herbert Simon's bounded rationality theorem from 1955, which states that due to limitations in the processing of information, people cannot act entirely rationally. Further, there is a tendency that depending on how the information is presented, people choose differently although according to the theory of expected utility, the alternatives are the same. This behaviour is referred to as a framing process in descriptive decision theory, a terminology introduced by Amos Tversky and Daniel Kahneman in 1986. Another violation of the expected utility decision rule (elaborated on in Chapter 3) occurs when gains are replaced by losses in choosing between alternatives with uncertain outcomes; people tend to be less keen on risk-taking when there are gains involved rather than losses. This was noted by Harry Markowitz already in 1952.

As mentioned already in the preface, another perspective is that of the normative kind. The aim of normative decision theory is to stipulate various decision formalisms and rules implying rational decision-making when followed. In this case, the logical foundations and the validity of the model do certainly matter. The proponents of such models often argue for them by constructing thought systems (sometimes called axiom systems) and from them deduce decision rules, which if correctly applied would result in a (normative) ordering of a set of available alternatives that a rational decision-maker is supposed to accept.

Prescriptive decision theory is, however, a more recent approach. The prescriptive theory focuses on identifying the discrepancies between how decisions are made (descriptive) and how the normative theory suggests that they should be made. One purpose of this theory is to bridge the gap between decision analysis and actual decision-making. The area of prescriptive decision methods is clearly derived from both the normative and descriptive kinds of decision theory but contains many elements of its own as well. For example, it contains approaches that deal with prescribing ways for the actual structuring and analysis of decision situations. A salient idea is to model the situations according to a structured model. Presuming the decision-maker to be reasonably rational, the prescriptive model can devise suitable courses of action, given the information supplied. This book will explore that idea and suggest suitable practical rules, processes, and thought patterns to follow in order to become a better decision-maker.

2

DECISION MODELLING

Traditional decision theory deals with only one decision-making part, one "player." The environment is considered neutral, and the probabilities of events are not affected by some conscious opponent. The only "opponent" is often referred to as nature. Game theory, on the other hand, introduces opponents to the decision situation. This means that the possibilities of consequences occurring depend on the acts of both the player and his opponent(s). Many complicated dependencies can arise, and only in special cases there are simple solutions to game problems. This book does not deal with game theory, instead only concentrating on decision theory and its applications to real-life decision situations.

Many aspects of decision-making are to a large extent qualitative, like the discovery and formulation of the problem itself. Searching for and gathering information also requires deliberate choices, as does the compilation of the information into a number of alternative courses of action. In other words, there is a soft side to any decision process. Quantitative information is abundant in almost all types of decisions. Often when something is being (numerically) assessed, the different alternatives are given monetary or other numeric values. On the basis of the given values, and perhaps on estimated (subjective) probabilities for the events, decisions are made using (hopefully) a decision rule but sometimes only a rule of thumb or the repetition of an old decision.

The terminology used within decision theory does not always correspond to the mundane interpretations of some concepts. Within decision theory, strict uncertainty refers to a situation where no information is available regarding the different probabilities of the states. In situations where some probability information is available, either as subjective (estimated) or objective (measured) probabilities, the term risk is used. An event is something discernible occurring at

DOI: 10.1201/9781003406709-2
11

a certain moment and should not be confused with a state which is something observable and constant over a period of time. A decision-maker chooses a course of action (alternative), and this choice results in a consequence which is the result of an event occurring after a deliberate choice of a course of action. The consequences of each alternative in the model are exhaustive and exclusive. Exhaustive means that the consequences together cover all possible cases in the modelled situation and exclusive means that every outcome belongs to only one consequence. Note that this is a property of your choice to model the situation. There are always unlikely outcomes that you have to exclude from your modelling in order for the model not to become too large to handle. For example, modelling three market scenarios for a product in a new market, the outcome "the entire company will go bankrupt" is probably an event you choose not to include. While on the other hand, if you have a company in a dire financial situation and you are the CEO, you probably will include the very same consequence as a highly relevant outcome. Thus, what does and does not constitute appropriate events to include is a modelling choice and depends on the situation and the decision problem you are approaching.

A decision situation can be modelled as having different possible future states, and, in most situations, it is beyond the capabilities of a decision-maker to tell in advance which state will become the true state. In this situation, the decision-maker is an entity facing a choice between a set of alternatives. Every alternative in turn has a set of consequences connected to the states via the alternatives, i.e. given an alternative and a state, there is a consequence of the selected alternative. The concern of the decision-maker is to choose the best alternative, given the sets of consequences and states. Given this, there are at least four basic types of difficulties:

- How should the decision-maker estimate the probabilities that the given states occur, given that a certain action is performed?
- How should the decision-maker estimate the different values of the consequences?
- How should the decision-maker compare the alternatives with respect to different multiple objectives on the decision?

- How should the decision-maker compare the alternatives for each objective?

The two latter concern multi-criteria decisions which we will address from Chapter 5 onwards. If we for the moment do not consider multiple objectives, a decision table such as the one in Table 2.1 is a frequently used representation of this kind of decision problem.

The possible states $(S_1, \ldots, S_n)$ describe a set of mutually exclusive (disjoint) and complete descriptions of the world, not leaving any relevant state out. These determine the consequences (such as C_{ij}) of the different alternatives $(A_1, \ldots, A_m)$. The true state is the state that does in fact occur. Thus, if the decision-maker selects alternative A_2 and if S_3 would then become the true state, consequence C_{23} will occur.

As stated above, various decision models exist for a number of different purposes. These models can be divided into three categories. The categories described differ with respect to their assumptions of the predictability of the future. In the risk-free (deterministic) world, there is no doubt about future events and all decisions can be made with certainty. In the strictly uncertain world, there are a number of possible scenarios but their respective probabilities are not taken into account. Finally, in the risky world, both different outcomes and their probabilities are taken into account when a good course of action is sought. In 1957, Duncan Luce and Howard Raiffa provided a useful classification of decision situations, addressing that an important factor in every decision problem is the decision-maker's knowledge and beliefs about the situation. They distinguished between the following three types of decision situations:

- Decisions under certainty
- Decisions under strict uncertainty
- Decisions under risk

Table 2.1 A Decision Table

	S_1	S_2	$\ldots$	S_n
A_1	C_{11}	C_{12}	$\ldots$	C_{1n}
A_2	C_{21}	C_{22}	$\ldots$	C_{2n}
$\ldots$	$\ldots$	$\ldots$	$\ldots$	$\ldots$
A_m	C_{m1}	C_{m2}	$\ldots$	C_{mn}

We will now discuss these three cases in turn (with the third one being presented in Chapter 3).

2.1 Decisions under Certainty

In decisions under certainty, the decision-maker knows the true state before he or she performs an action or can predict the consequences with certainty. This means that there is only one state column in the decision table for this kind of decision (cf. Table 2.1). Thus, in this case, it is reasonable to demand of a rational decision-maker that he or she should choose the alternative whose one and only consequence has a value not less than the value of any other alternative. This simple case requires no decision method and does rarely occur in important real-life decision-making situations.

2.2 Decisions under Strict Uncertainty

Within decision theory, strict uncertainty is defined as the situation appearing when a number of courses of action are possible and the decision-maker has no estimates of the probabilities of the different states. Then, it only remains to consider the outcomes of the states and make a decision based on them.

A special case of strict uncertainty modelling, used for quite some time and still in use in everyday situations, is the analysis of argumentation. It refers to writing down the advantages and the disadvantages of each alternative in pro and contra lists. The advantages are then weighted against the disadvantages, and the most favourable alternative is chosen. The defensively inclined decision-maker will instead of choosing the most favourable rather choose the alternative avoiding as many disadvantages as possible. We will discuss this technique in Chapter 6 on the Pilot Method.

In decisions under strict uncertainty, the decision-maker cannot quantify his or her uncertainty in any way; thus, no probability estimates are possible to make. John Milnor did, in 1954, provide an exposition of four proposals for decision rules by four different authors:

- The Principle of Insufficient Reason (Laplace, 1816)
- The Maximin Principle (Wald, 1950)

- The Pessimism-Optimism Index (Hurwicz, 1951)
- The Minimax-Regret Principle (Savage, 1951)

The decision rule of Laplace is based on the assumption that if the probabilities of the different states are completely unknown, then they can be assumed to be equal. This idea is commonly referred to as the principle of insufficient reason. Choose the alternative that has the highest average value of the possible outcomes. In Table 2.2, this corresponds to the largest average across the rows, yielding A_1 as the best alternative at

$$\frac{2+2+0+1}{4} = 1.25$$

Wald's principle can be expressed as follows. For each alternative (row in the table), mark the consequence with the lowest outcome value. Then, select the alternative with the highest marked outcome value. As can be seen, Wald's view on strict uncertainty was not an optimistic one since according to Wald, you should always choose the alternative that gives the best result if the worst possible outcome would occur for each alternative. Therefore, it was coined the maximin utility criterion and originated from Wald's work in game theory. In Table 2.2, this corresponds to the largest minimum value across the rows, with A_2 as the best alternative having 1 as its lowest outcome.

As a reaction to Wald, the rule of Hurwicz has a less pessimistic approach. Hurwicz recommends a mixture of a pessimistic and an optimistic attitude. Mark the worst outcome for each alternative in red (same as in Wald's rule). Then, do the opposite and mark the best outcome for each alternative in blue. Choose a constant k between 0 and 1 as the pessimism-optimism index with higher numbers being more pessimistic. Then, calculate $k \cdot$ red value $+ (1-k) \cdot$ blue value for each alternative and select the one with the highest sum. Note that if you select $k = 1$, this is again Wald's maximin utility criterion (most

Table 2.2 Milnor's Example

	S_1	S_2	S_3	S_4	
A_1	20	20	0	10	Alternative chosen by Laplace
A_2	10	10	10	10	Alternative chosen by Wald
A_3	0	40	0	0	Alternative chosen by Hurwicz (with $k > 1/4$)
A_4	10	30	0	0	Alternative chosen by Savage

pessimistic), whereas if you select $k = 0$, it is the so-called maximax utility criterion (most optimistic). In Table 2.2, this corresponds to a combination of the largest maximum and minimum values across the rows. For values of k larger than 0.25, say $k = 0.5$, this yields A_3 as the best alternative at $(0.5 \cdot 4) + (0.5 \cdot 0) = 2$.

In statistician Leonard Savage's own words from 1972: "[...] the minimax-regret rule recommends the choice of such an act that the greatest loss that can possibly accrue to it shall be as small as possible." Thus, the decision-maker should choose the alternative giving the smallest possible "regret." To arrive at that, for each possible state mark the best possible alternative. Then for each outcome in each alternative, calculate the difference between the outcome and the best one, i.e. the regret you experience for each state if you picked the wrong alternative. In Table 2.2, this corresponds to the smallest difference across the rows, with A_4 as the best alternative having a difference of 1 as its worst outcome. This *minimax-regret criterion* was originally suggested as an improvement over Wald's maximin utility criterion.

Coming back to Milnor, he produced a simple example where all of the four seemingly reasonable decision rules yield different results. Table 2.2 shows Milnor's example where, as an illustration, assume that the numbers are thousands of dollars you receive in a game where a card is drawn from a deck of cards and its suit (club = S_1, diamond = S_2, heart = S_3, or spade = S_4) determines the amount of money you receive. Which alternative should you choose?

We will, in Chapter 8, give you guidelines for which rules to pick in these and other kinds of decision situations. As a further numerical example of these decision rules, consider the following example.

Example 2.1: The owner of an ice cream parlour at an ocean waterfront is considering the planning options for the upcoming year. The season consists mostly of the summer months, but to be effective, plans need to be decided well in advance. Until last year, the parlour was the only one in the neighbourhood, but rumour has it that a competitor is moving in. As the owner sees it, one of three scenarios (states) will occur: she will be alone on the market again next year (S_1), another parlour of a similar kind will establish itself in the area (S_2), or a super parlour will be built by investors having much more money at their disposal (S_3). Ignorant of the true state, the owner must decide what to do with her own parlour. She has three options: she does nothing to her parlour (A_1), she modernises it (A_2), or she expands it into a bigger establishment, though not as big as a super parlour (A_3). The income matrix in dollars is given in Table 2.3.

Table 2.3 Parlour Income Matrix

	S_1	S_2	S_3
DO NOTHING (A_1)	180,000	135,000	55,000
MODERNISE (A_2)	230,000	160,000	70,000
EXPAND (A_3)	300,000	210,000	105,000

The cost of modernising the parlour is $30,000, and an expansion costs $60,000. The net income matrix, adjusted for building costs, is given in Table 2.4. The rules described will be applied to this example to aid the understanding of them.

Table 2.4 Parlour Net Income Matrix

	S_1	S_2	S_3
DO NOTHING (A_1)	180,000	135,000	55,000
MODERNISE (A_2)	200,000	130,000	40,000
EXPAND (A_3)	240,000	150,000	45,000

Above, we saw that Wald's maximin rule stems from a desire to constrain the unfavourable outcomes and is thus a defensive rule. More precisely, the course of action is sought that is the least unwanted, should the worst occur. This way, the decision-maker ensures that the outcome has the best guaranteed minimal outcome level. For decisions where an individual or organisation is sensitive to failures, this might be a good strategy.

The minimal profits from each alternative all occur in state S_3, when a super parlour is established. The maximal entry in column S_3 is A_1, which then is the preferred alternative by the maximin rule. This is summarised in Table 2.5.

Table 2.5 Parlour Minimum Net Income

	MIN
DO NOTHING (A_1)	50,000
MODERNISE (A_2)	40,000
EXPAND (A_3)	45,000

Maximax is another decision rule that has the opposite aim of maximin. As the name suggests, the decision-maker seeks to maximise the best outcome, which is an offensive strategy. In other words, the alternative is chosen whose most favourable outcome is the highest of all. For decisions where an individual or organisation is in great need of successful outcomes, this can be a good strategy.

The maximal profits from each alternative all occur in state S_1, when no other parlour is established. The maximal entry in column S_1 is A_3, which then is the preferred alternative by the maximax rule. This is summarised in Table 2.6.

Table 2.6   Parlour Maximum Net Income

	MAX
DO NOTHING (A_1)	180,000
MODERNISE (A_2)	200,000
EXPAND (A_3)	240,000

Both maximin and maximax are in some sense extreme alternatives. An attempt to choose the golden mean is the Hurwicz rule discussed earlier. Recall that it tries to consider the weighted average of the least favourable and the most favourable outcomes for each alternative using a weight factor k between 0 and 1 that can be thought of as a risk index. As we saw, emerging as special cases, Hurwicz' rule turns into maximax for $k = 0$ and into maximin for $k = 1$. Thus, it is a generalisation of the rules above and when employing the rule, it is important to select the risk factor k corresponding to your risk profile, something considered in Chapter 8.

The minimal profits from each alternative are 50, 40, and 45, respectively, and the maximal profits are 180, 200, and 240. Applying those numbers to Hurwicz' rule, for the parameter k between 0 and 0.86, A_3 is the preferred alternative, and for k between 0.86 and 1, A_1 is instead preferred. Since we know that $k = 0$ is the maximax rule and $k = 1$ is maximin, those results coincide with earlier parts of the example.

The question remains: to act rationally, which one of the above rules should be employed? Are there any criteria by which decision rules such as the above ones can be judged? Milnor suggested a set of ten criteria, of which the following are the most important ones.

- *Complete ranking*: The rule should give a complete ranking among the alternatives.
- *Value scale independence*: The result should not change if all values are multiplied by the same number.
- *Strong domination*: The rule should prefer an alternative that is superior in all states.

- *Irrelevance independence*: The result should not change if you add an irrelevant alternative.
- *Constant independence*: The result should not change if you add a constant to a column.
- *Row permutation independence*: The result should not change if you change the order of the rows.
- *Column duplication independence*: The result should not change if you duplicate a column.

Somewhat surprisingly, Milnor showed that no decision rule can comply with all of these seemingly reasonable requirements. Hence, we have this set of rules for decisions under strict uncertainty, none of which can universally be agreed on as being *the* rule. As it later turned out, it was shown that it is indeed impossible to find a decision rule that fulfils all the desired properties. Perhaps the last requirement, that of column duplication independence, is too strong. If the decision matrix changes, the entire decision problem could be seen as having changed into a new one. Then, it might not be surprising that decision rules such as these run into trouble. Excluding that requirement, Laplace's rule does indeed satisfy all the other requirements. We saw earlier in this chapter that this rule is based on the implicit assumption that uncertainty is the same as assigning equal probabilities to all states. This assumption is usually attributed to Laplace, hence its name, and constitutes a link between methods for making decisions under strict uncertainty (this chapter) and methods for making decisions under risk (Chapter 3). Laplace's rule is similar to maximising the expected value when all probabilities are assigned the same number.

3

BAYESIAN DECISION ANALYSIS

In real-life decision situations, it is rather unusual for there to be no information available at all on the probabilities involved. Therefore, it seems to be a plausible extension of the decision rules in the previous chapter to try to incorporate more of the information actually available into the decision process. However, in the defence of the strict uncertainty models from the previous chapter, it can be noted that they provide a good overview of a decision situation and are sometimes good enough of an approximation of the situation to make a decision. Thus, they are by no means useless, they rather constitute a first level of decision, analysis, and we now proceed to the next level. We will discuss on how to choose the appropriate modelling level in Chapter 8.

When the decision-maker is able to quantify his or her beliefs in terms of probabilities, given a course of action, it is said that the decision is made under risk. If all probabilities and values (utilities) in a decision problem are subjectively assigned numerical values by the decision-maker, and then the problem is evaluated according to the principle of maximising the expected utility, the decision-maker uses Bayesian decision analysis, named after the English clergyman Thomas Bayes mentioned in Chapter 1.

Although, as we saw in Chapter 1, the theories of probability can be traced back to the 16th century, the foundations of modern probability theory were laid by Andrey Kolmogorov (1903–1987). He rigorously constructed a probability theory and defined the concept of conditional expectation (i.e. the probabilities of sequences of events) in *Grundbegriffe der Wahrscheinlichkeitsrechnung* (1933) and in *Analytic Methods in Probability Theory* (1938).

Let us now take a closer look at some of the constituent components of modern rational decision-making and elaborate on parts of the terminology introduced earlier. We begin with the concepts of

DOI: 10.1201/9781003406709-3
21

probability and utility (or value) which, when combined, make up the expected utility/value. Any event that is not certain to occur is a matter of some uncertainty. When a decision-maker has to act in situations where uncertainty prevails, and this uncertainty can be quantified in terms of a probability, it is said that the decision is made under risk. In Bayesian decision theory, probabilities are used to capture and model beliefs. Thus, they are considered to be measures of degrees of belief. If possible, performing statistical investigations to obtain these degrees of beliefs is good, but in most real-life situations, historical data is not available and the probability assessments have to be made on more subjective grounds.

A basic statement of probability regards an event E and takes a form such as "the probability of the uncertain event E is p," where p is a real number between 0 and 1 (0% and 100%) inclusive, where 0% denotes that the event is totally impossible and 100% denotes that the event is guaranteed to occur. For example, E can be the statement "it will not rain on your next birthday and you will receive at least ten gifts." The probability of all events that are modelled in a decision situation must sum exactly to 1 (100%) since it is certain (in the model) that one of the events in the decision situation (the so-called sample space) will be the true outcome, i.e. this is the condition of exhaustiveness. This is a model prerequisite also for the models in Chapter 2, although there numbers are not assigned to the probabilities of events occurring. It is important to note that events not modelled by the decision-maker have a probability of exactly 0% in the model but might occur in real life if the model is incomplete (which is almost always is; this is both the advantage and disadvantage of a model – it covers all reasonable cases but not the rest of the outcomes such as a meteorite falling from the sky). Further, conditional probabilities arise when additional information is obtained such as "the probability of E given that F already occurred." Thus, the decision-maker knows that F has occurred and this might have an impact on the probability of E. For example, in medical applications, a test yields a positive result which in turn implies some probability of an actual disease.

The examples so far have in a sense been simplified, in that all alternatives had the same outcomes. But in real-life decisions, the same number of consequences (states) does not always belong to each alternative. Rather, in actual decision situations, it is common for the number of consequences to differ between alternatives within the same decision problem. The risk matrices of the previous chapter can be modified to take care of this, but a tree representation is often both more natural and more perspicuous. And besides, graphical models often have an intuitive appeal to humans. They serve well as an instrument for communication since they are dynamic and easy to understand and modify.

Howard Raiffa is commonly credited for the first use of decision trees in 1968. A decision tree has three different types of nodes: decision nodes, event nodes (chance nodes), and consequence nodes. In a decision tree, usually squares represent decisions to be made (decision nodes) and circles represent chance events (event nodes). The edges emanating from a square represent the identified alternatives or the choices available to the decision-maker, and the edges from an event node represent the possible outcomes of a chance event with an associated probability distribution. The third decision element, the consequence, is specified at the leaves as consequence nodes. These are associated with a real numbered value representing the utilities of the different consequences. An example of a decision tree is shown in Figure 3.1.

In a decision node, the decision-maker selects one of a number of courses of action, and following this decision, there are chance (or random) nodes. Chance nodes can be regarded as nodes in which nature chooses one of its available "courses of action." Larger decision models become clearer if the decision situations are represented in tree form.

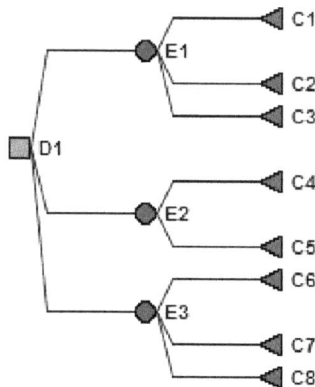

Figure 3.1 A decision tree.

In some applications, the decisions are made in several distinct steps. The tree then indicates a temporal order in which the events take place, with those to the left occurring first, and thus, time progresses rightwards. Any decision problem in tree form can be transformed into a problem in normal form. Being in normal form means that the decision situation can be modelled and evaluated in the following way.

- First, the player (= the decision-maker) selects one alternative from all alternatives available to him.
- Thereafter, nature selects one outcome from the available set of consequences, whose members might be dependent on the player's previous selection.

The decision-maker's choice is made from the available set of courses of action, and it is assumed that he or she understands what the alternatives mean. It is also assumed that the decision-maker is rational in the sense that he or she is determined to choose the preferred alternative according to his or her decision rule. Further, the tree and matrix forms of presenting a decision problem are representationally equivalent. Therefore, it is sufficient to model decision problems in normal form.

We have seen that risk is defined as the situation where a number of courses of action are available and the decision-maker has some estimates of the probabilities of the states involved. Usually, the probabilities are not equal for each alternative as they were found to be in Laplace's rule in Chapter 2. There, the matrix form was an easy way to represent strict uncertainty models. Risk situations can also be modelled using matrix models. The matrices are similar, but they are amended with a new row containing a probability for each state.

Consider a decision situation with two alternatives (A_1 and A_2) and two states common to both alternatives (S_1 and S_2). For each of the four possibilities, a value is assigned. For each state, a probability is also assigned. This probability might be based on a series of experiments or observations. The decision situation is then observed many times, and the number of times each state is obtained is recorded. Based on the fractions of occurrence, every state is assigned a probability. More commonly, the probabilities have to be estimated by the decision-maker. Subjective estimates are used when for one reason or another it is expensive, hard, or even impossible to obtain objective

Table 3.1 Decision Matrix for Decisions under Risk

	STATE		
	S_1	S_2	
PROBABILITIES	p_1	p_2	
ALTERNATIVE A_1	v_{11}	v_{12}	$E(A_1) = p_1 \cdot v_{11} + p_2 \cdot v_{12}$
ALTERNATIVE A_2	v_{21}	v_{22}	$E(A_2) = p_1 \cdot v_{21} + p_2 \cdot v_{22}$

probabilities for the events. The matrix for two alternatives by two states is shown in Table 3.1.

The rules for deciding the preferred alternative in this model are not as simple as before. The usage of strict uncertainty rules from the previous chapter disregards any prevailing probability information. If such information is available, though, it seems wise to use it and try to calculate representative aggregated values for the courses of action. Taking the direct mean values would again disregard the given information, and this leads to the idea of assigning weights to the values depending on how probable they are, i.e. calculating the expected value. In Table 3.1, it can be seen how the expected values $E(A_1)$ and $E(A_2)$ are calculated for both alternatives where the letter E stands for expectancy and the label within parenthesis is the alternative being calculated. The alternative having the largest expected value is the alternative expected to be the most favourable choice for the decision-maker. The decision principle of maximising the expected value has the advantage of being relatively easy to calculate as long as the probabilities and values are fixed real numbers.

Example 3.1: Recall the ice cream parlour from Example 2.2. By talking to officials at the city council, the parlour owner now has access to information regarding how probable the scenarios really are. Her estimates of the probabilities are included in the expanded table (Table 3.2).

Table 3.2 Parlour Net Income Matrix with Probabilities

	S_1	S_2	S_3	$E(A_i)$
STATE PROBABILITY	25%	40%	35%	
DO NOTHING (A_1)	180,000	125,000	50,000	118,250
MODERNISE (A_2)	200,000	115,000	40,000	116,000
EXPAND (A_3)	210,000	120,000	35,000	135,750

The expected values are now easily calculated according to the rule and entered into the table. The results indicate that alternative A_3 is clearly better than A_1 and A_2.

Moving on to decision trees, they are usually evaluated by "pruning" the tree, sometimes called "rolling back" or "folding back" the tree. Start at the consequence nodes at the far right and move left towards the root node. Calculate the expected values of chance nodes when such are encountered and replace the chance node with its expected value. When a decision node is encountered, choose the branch with the highest value, discarding other branches with lower expected values. When this procedure terminates, the path that remains is the one to choose. A deep tree is often, however, a bit too complicated for manual calculations, and we recommend using a computer program if you have such deep trees, i.e. with events following each other in sequence.

The tree indicates the temporal order in which events take place, i.e. in Figure 3.1, if event E4 is to occur before E3, then E4 is placed to the left of E4 in the model since time flows from left to right. This is especially important to notice if there is more than one decision node, i.e. all outcomes related to preceding nodes must be known prior to the actual decision the decision node represents. Furthermore, the tree is a representation of a conditional probability order. For example, the probability of C1 in Figure 3.1 is a conditional probability since it is conditional on the probability of the event E1. This is a bit complicated to calculate using pen and paper. Thus, the guidelines in Chapter 8 will ask you to use a computer program if you have sequences (chains) of events, i.e. more than one level of events in the tree and possibly sub-decisions in between.

As we have now seen, a reasonable decision rule for decisions under risk is the principle of maximing the expected value (PMEV). Under the assumption that the decision-maker is risk-neutral, this is a plausible and rather straightforward rule. Risk neutrality is a concept from utility theory, meaning that the decision-maker regards a certain sum of money twice as desirable as half that amount. This rule has been the subject of debates within decision theory and economics as well as philosophy.

Example 3.2: A person must choose between receiving $5,000 and participating in a lottery where the probability of winning $10,000 is exactly 50% and the probability of winning nothing at all is also exactly

50%. According to a rule based on the expected monetary value, the two options have exactly the same value – they are both worth $5,000. Suppose that the person is in immediate need of surgery at the cost of $4,000 to save his life. If the money is not available by any other means, having $5,000 for sure is worth much more than the chance of winning $10,000, virtually regardless of the probabilities involved. If, on the other hand, the surgery carries the price tag of $8,000, then receiving $5,000 is of little interest, whereas a 50% chance of receiving $10,000 translates to a 50% chance of surviving.

Most people not being in such a dire situation would choose the $5,000 for sure which is known as the sure-thing principle, i.e. a propensity to select an alternative that has a certain outcome if it is as good as other prospects. The purpose of this overly colourful example is to point out the possibility that the monetary value of an action does not necessarily correspond to the real value in all situations for all individuals or organisations. If the monetary values exactly correspond to proportional utilities, it is easy to map them directly onto the utility scale which then assumes the same function as a monetary scale. Henceforth in this book, the generic concept of value will apply to utilities, monetary values, or other values.

The term utility can be regarded as a measure of some degree of satisfaction, and a utility assigns to outcomes, i.e. losses or gains, numbers representing this degree of satisfaction. The utility function defined by Bernoulli was considered adequate for almost 200 years. However, Karl Menger (1902–1985) showed in his *Das Unsicherheitsmoment in der Wertlehre* (1934) that the Bernoulli function was heuristic and ad hoc and further that the function was unsatisfactory already on formal grounds. Also in 1934, Menger showed the existence of a game related to the game presented in the St. Petersburg Paradox, in which the subjective expectation of the gambler on the basis of this value function is infinite when evaluating additions to a fortune by any unbounded function. The implication of this is that it is always possible to provide a paradox, equivalent to the St. Petersburg Paradox, which cannot be resolved only through the idea of diminishing marginal utility. Menger further showed the inadequacy of mathematical utility functions of the type suggested by Bernoulli's contemporary mathematician Gabriel Cramer (1704–1752).

In general, people are willing to pay more money for what they consider to be more desirable. In this respect, a monetary scale can at least function as an ordinal scale, i.e. a scale where higher numbers signify more desirable outcomes but without the possibility to state the magnitudes of desire, i.e. a plain ordering. For a majority of business decisions, the use of monetary scales is considered a reasonable and acceptable measure of utility. However, it is not uncommon that monetary values are used as proxies for non-monetary outcomes, such as public health and environmental damage.

Utility theory was not, at the time of Menger's results, a well-founded subject. That situation prevailed until the late 1930s and early 1940s when the works of Frank Ramsey, John von Neumann, and Oskar Morgenstern appeared. They are credited for the formal foundation of utility theory. They proposed reasonable principles governing decisions, out of which they constructed a theory where a set of basic assumptions (called axioms) was formulated to justify the utility principle. One idea was to, in a systematic way, define the meaning of rationality. The point was that if a decision rule can be deduced from an indisputable chain of reasoning, then this rule should be the natural and obvious rule for a rational decision-maker provided that the necessary information is available.

The discussion so far seems safe and sound enough, but are people rational in the sense that PMEV presupposes, or can they even be that? PMEV is convenient in several ways, but it must still be functional for ordinary people in order to be prescriptively useful. And is it really a reasonable concept of rationality despite the fact that normative researchers consider it to be a definition of rationality?

Consider the reasons for gambling. Many people would agree that there is some kind of pleasure involved in the act of participating in a game with uncertain outcomes. If the mathematical expectation was the only criterion for gambling, no games would ever be arranged by rational beings since when the rules of the game would make it rational for the gambler to bet, then the arranger should be irrational to offer the bet, and vice versa. However, people do still arrange and participate in games although either the gambler or the bookmaker will be on the irrational side. Furthermore, it has also been argued that humans tend to disregard very small probabilities, even in games with finite mathematical expectations (like nationwide lotteries), and also that, in the case of very high probabilities, a gambler is not willing to risk arbitrary amounts.

The case can be made that people find pleasure and excitement in gambling and are thus prepared to break what they know is rational, i.e. staying in line with PMEV. This is not a bad thing in itself. We guess that every reader of this book has one time or another acted in a way they knew was not rational or optimal but made a lot of sense, given the fun or the pleasure involved. We are not doing anything actually bad here, but just maybe having that extra piece of cake that was not entirely justified on any rational grounds, given the factual situation.

The suggestion that the PMEV is logically sufficient, and the question of whether it reflects the properties of a rational decision-maker, has not passed without criticism or debate. Proponents of classical Bayesian decision theory often argue that the concept of utility captures different risk attitudes. The assumption is that to each expected utility, there corresponds a certainty monetary equivalent. The decision-maker is indifferent between having this monetary value with certainty and pursuing an alternative with uncertain outcomes but with the same expected value. The risk premium of an action is now stated as the amount that a decision-maker requires for carrying out the act instead of having the monetary equivalent for certain. With respect to the risk premium, a classification of decision-makers into three classes can be made: a decision-maker is risk-averse if the premium is positive, risk-prone if the premium is negative, and risk-neutral if the premium is zero.

Continuing that line of thought, in 1984, philosopher Dagfinn Føllesdal suggested the following requirements for a reasonable decision rule:

- A decision rule should recommend an alternative with valuable consequences before an alternative with less valuable consequences.
- A decision rule should recommend an alternative with a high probability of valuable consequences before an alternative with a low probability of valuable consequences.
- A decision rule should recommend an alternative with a lower probability of bad consequences before an alternative with a higher probability of bad consequences.

This indeed seems to be reasonable, but it might be a bit too vague to fill the needs of decision theory, and thus, it has been elaborated on by researchers in utility theory. Several elaborations exist, but they have all been subject to controversies. Human decision-makers tend to, under given circumstances, behave inconsistently with respect to the utility principle. Famous so-called paradoxes include Allais' paradox and Ellsberg's paradox which we will investigate against the backdrop of the sure-thing principle, coined by Leonard Savage.

> A businessman contemplates buying a certain piece of property. He considers the outcome of the next presidential election relevant. So, to clarify the matter to himself, he asks whether he would buy if he knew that the Democratic candidate were going to win, and decides that he would. Similarly, he considers whether he would buy if he knew that the Republican candidate were going to win, and again finds that he would. Seeing that he would buy in either event, he decides that he should buy, even though he does not know which event obtains, or will obtain, as we would ordinarily say.
>
> **Savage (1954)**

In Allais' paradox from 1953, people are offered to participate in one of two lotteries, each having 100 lottery tickets of which a person is to draw one. Lottery A gives $100,000 for each of the 100 tickets. Lottery B gives $500,000 on 10 tickets, $100,000 on 89 tickets, and 0 on the last ticket. Most people, but not all, choose lottery A because of the certainty to receive a large sum of money (assuming this is indeed a large sum for them). Next, the same persons are given a new offer of participating in one of two other lotteries. Lottery C has $1 million on 11 tickets and 0 on the remaining 89, while Lottery D has $5 million on 10 tickets and 0 on the remaining 90. This time, most people choose Lottery D because of its higher reward on the non-zero tickets. According to PMEV, though, you should have picked A over B and C over D, or B over A and D over C. This is regardless of the utility you assign to the money as can be seen in Table 3.3 where the tickets are numbered 1–100 and the contents of tickets 1–89, 90–99, and 100, respectively, are in different columns. The only difference between the pairs A–B

Table 3.3 Allais' Paradox

TICKET	1–89	90–99	100
LOTTERY A	100,000	100,000	100,000
LOTTERY B	100,000	500,000	0
LOTTERY C	0	100,000	100,000
LOTTERY D	0	500,000	0

and C–D is that $100,000 have been deducted equally from lotteries C and D for tickets 1–89. Thus, Allais' paradox shows that people tend to act inconsistent with respect to PMEV. The paradox draws on the sure-thing principle, a common human behaviour of preferring a good outcome for certain to having a chance situation between something not as good and something even better.

In Ellsberg's paradox from 1961, people were offered a choice between participating in different gambles. They are based on two urns, U1 and U2, with 100 balls each in them. In U1, 50 balls are red and the other 50 are black. People are then offered two gambles, both consisting of drawing one ball from the urn without seeing its colour. In gamble A, you receive $10,000 if the ball is red and nothing otherwise, while in gamble B, you receive $10,000 if the ball is black and nothing otherwise. Next, there is an offer to participate in two other gambles involving the urn U2, also with 100 red and black balls but this time in an unknown mix. Again, in gamble C, you receive $10,000 if the ball is red and nothing otherwise, while in gamble D you receive $10,000 if the ball is black and nothing otherwise. Most people are indifferent between gambles A or B while preferring both of them to C or D even though the expected utility of all gambles are the same. Thus, the Ellsberg paradox is quite similar to Allais' in that it shows people's tendencies towards preferring known risks to unknown uncertainties and thereby violating the utility principle. While this was not Ellsberg's terminology, from a prescriptive point of view, we observe that the probabilities in A and B are objective ones while we deal with subjective probabilities in C and D.

Paradoxes of these kinds are often seemingly resolved by arguing that even intelligent beings make mistakes and after some explanation of the inconsistency in their choices, they change their minds.

However, for instance, an empirical study in 1974 by Paul Slovic and Amos Tversky showed that as much as about 30% of the decision-makers – even after having been told about and understood their decision mistake – refused to change their opinion in order to conform to the expected value principle. Following up, Tversky tried in 1981 to find out why this is the case, and his conclusion was that irrelevant contextual effects are often influencing people, making them act inconsistent with the utility principle, i.e. the problem lies mostly in the framing process. Further, it can be argued that it is impossible for any normative theory of decision-making to embrace all inherent peculiarities in a free world of heterogeneous decision-making inhabitants. This again points to the prescriptive perspective as being the only practical way forward.

The information to which the PMEV is to be applied must be of such a nature that it can meaningfully represent people's preferences, provided that these are consistent. For instance, several cognitive and behavioural biases play a role in the decision-making processes. One such is connected with risk perceptions under conditions of ambiguity such as the paradoxes discussed above. There are also availability cascades, i.e. individuals adopt a new insight since other people have adopted it, the availability heuristic, the misunderstanding of frequency of occurrence, and the ease with which especially recent examples come to mind. Further, there are bandwagon effects and information cascades, where individual adoption is strongly correlated to the proportion of people who have already adopted an idea, combined with the enormous amount of available information. The list can go on and on, continuing with the base rate fallacy, probability neglects, exaggerated expectations, framing problems, group thinking in general, and many others, but this is not a book on descriptive decision theory, so we will limit ourselves to mentioning a few. The interested reader can easily find information on a large set of biases since we in this book focus less on descriptive features and, while heeding them, rather focus on ways forward because ultimately, we need to make decisions by making the best use of whatever information we have available. Another culprit factor is bounded rationality when individuals are limited regarding their ability or willingness to collect information and are unable to identify an even perceived optimal solution, leading to decisions being made in a significantly simplified decision space, where the decision-makers must be content with a certain (again perceived) acceptable level of performance. Decision-makers thus search, in this sense, for a satisfactory solution, but they focus only on a limited set of options from available alternatives. The remedy here, as in many other settings in life, is continuous experience. Practice makes perfect. The more you train, by using methods in this book to make decisions and then reflect on them, the better you become at decision-making in general and avoiding biases and bounded rationality in particular. Sometimes, of course, the outcome is not your desired one – nobody gets his or her favoured outcome all of the time – but the decision made given what you knew at the time might have been the best one anyway. This is what you should strive for.

In attempts to circumvent paradoxes and biases such as those above, researchers have tried to modify the application of PMEV, e.g. by bringing regret or disappointment into the evaluation to cover cases where numerically equivalent results are appreciated differently depending on what was once in someone's possession. Thus, researchers, not least within economics, have proposed a number of alternative decision rules to replace the PMEV. During the 1980s, many researchers tried to come up with modified PMEV-like rules to patch observed problems away. Peter Fishburn (1983) suggested an evaluation based on the quotient between two separate expected values. Graham Loomes and Robert Sugden (1982) brought regret or disappointment into the evaluation to cover cases where numerically equal results were appreciated differently depending on what was once in someone's possession. John Quiggin (1982) and Menahem Yaari (1987) independently tried to resolve the problems by requiring functions to modify the probabilities in the evaluation rule with a strictly increasing function. None of these suggestions, however, are without their own problems. Per-Erik Malmnäs showed in 1996 for those patches above and for some other similar proposals that their performances are at best almost equal to that of the expected value and at worst quite much poorer, e.g. not even being consistent with some very basic requirements for a rational decision rule. Thus, nothing has been gained by such patching attempts and the conclusion remains that all evaluation rules are subject to counterexamples similar to Allais' with no rule performing consistently better than the original expected value.

There seem to be no compelling reasons to altogether reject the use of the PMEV, but since there exists no absolutely rational decision rule, a reasonable decision method should provide possibilities for evaluating decision situations in several respects. In many decision contexts, decision-makers might wish to avoid particular alternatives that involve some risk of ending up in a consequence that is, for the decision-maker, considered a catastrophe, or at least highly undesirable. Even if the probability of such an event is estimated to be very low, it might simply not be a risk that the decision-maker is willing to be exposed to. An insurance company serves as a pertinent example since insurance companies surely find it irrational to let their clients insure themselves against nuclear war, meteorites, acts of terrorism, and similar catastrophes. Although the insurance company might find such events to be highly improbable, the occurrence of any such event would without doubt imply bankruptcy. One way to express such risk-averse attitudes is the ability to define security thresholds (often called security levels) that exclude alternatives having a too high probability (even if being low in absolute terms) for an outcome that has an unacceptably low value. This will be enlarged on in Chapters 4, 6, and 8.

Thus, within prescriptive decision analysis, having a more pragmatic approach than a purely normative theory of rational choice, the PMEV supplemented with security levels is deemed sufficient in order to serve as a valuable tool for comparing decision alternatives. This is the best we can do, and it is definitely good enough. This closes the debate from a prescriptive point of view and we can safely move on to the next topic, that of imprecise information.

4

IMPRECISE INFORMATION

In quite a few real-life decision situations, the decision-maker does not have access to the amount of information demanded to come up with precise numerical values and probabilities nor have the ability to make precise and accurate estimates of values. A great deal of attention has been given to the need for imprecise information as a source of decision uncertainty. In 1990, Millett Granger Morgan and Max Henrion identified two main types of uncertainty. The first type of uncertainty derives from a lack of historical data and includes statistical variation, subjective judgments, linguistic imprecision, variability, inherent randomness, disagreement, and approximation. For example, in experiments, errors in the measurements of quantities give rise to statistical variation. The second type of uncertainty arises from the model chosen, e.g. how to represent and express a utility function in a reasonably correct way. Furthermore, uncertainty due to biases in communication and value differences is unavoidable.

Thus, the decision-maker seldom has access to precise statements such as "with a 22% probability consequence C will occur." Often, he or she has no access at all to objective probabilities but has to resort to subjective probabilities. In many cases, a subjective probability does not possess enough precision to confidently yield a single, fixed number to describe the situation. A fixed number could give a false impression of accuracy, and yet, many methods work in this way because calculations become simpler. Another way would be to give imprecise probability statements, e.g. in the form of intervals, where the width of an interval reflects how sure the decision-maker is of that specific piece of information. The statement "the probability of consequence C is between 20% and 60%" is as good a statement as "the probability of consequence C is between 30% and 50%" in the sense that it reflects the decision-maker's capability and belief at the time of utterance. Statements such as "the probability of consequence C is quite high and the probability of consequence C is definitely low" are also plausible.

DOI: 10.1201/9781003406709-4
35

One main issue is also whether people really are capable of providing the inputs that utility theory requires. Traditional utility theory requires much background information that might not be accessible to decision-makers. In its standard form, it is assumed that the decision-maker can assign precise numerical values to the consequences as well as precise numerical probabilities, both with good precision. Humans are often incapable of providing the inputs that utility theory seems to require. Even if decision-makers can distinguish between different probabilities, it is still the case that complete, adequate, and accurate information often is lacking in decision situations. However, the notion of being able to rank different courses of action from most to least preferable by assigning values to different consequences is well-established. Instead, when trying to address real-world problems, where uncertainty about data prevails, there is a high degree of subjectivity in judgements. Therefore, models with representations allowing imprecise probability and value statements have been suggested in the literature.

4.1 Imprecise Probability

According to Peter Walley, most research in imprecise probabilities has been concerned with different types of upper and lower probability.

> Consider the uncertainty about whether it will rain in Brisbane next weekend. A weather forecaster may be able to assess a precise probability of rain, such as 0.3285…, although even an expert should feel uncomfortable about specifying a probability to more than one or two decimal places. Someone who has little information about the prospects for rain may be able to make only an imprecise judgement such as "it will probably rain," or "it is more likely to rain tomorrow than at the weekend," or "the probability of rain is between 0.2 and 0.4." People living outside Australia may be completely ignorant about the weather in Brisbane and assign lower probability 0 and upper probability 1. Probabilities based on extensive data can be distinguished, through their precision, from those based on ignorance.

Walley (1997)

Walley's highly influential *Statistical Reasoning with Imprecise Probabilities* from 1991 introduces the concept of upper and lower bounds to probabilities (which he calls previsions). Briefly speaking, the lower prevision of a gamble is defined by the amount a gambler is willing to pay for a lottery ticket and the upper prevision is defined by how much he or she is willing to sell the same ticket for.

According to the philosophers Peter Gärdenfors and Nils-Erik Sahlin, one of the major disadvantages of the classic Bayesian approach is that it does not account for variations of the epistemic reliability in different decision situations. Even if an outcome is associated with a set of probability measures and a set of utility measures, some of these measures are often regarded as more reliable than others due to the nature of the obtained information. Thus, we have a second-order belief in the sense that we hold some of our beliefs to be more reliable. Gärdenfors and Sahlin provide an example for demonstrating variations in the epistemic reliability in which Miss Julie is invited to bet on the winner of three different tennis matches:

> As regards match A, she is very well-informed about the two players – she knows everything about the results of their earlier matches, she has watched them play several times, she is familiar with their present physical condition and the setting of the match, etc. Given all this information, Miss Julie predicts that it will be a very even match and that a mere chance will determine the winner. In match B, she knows nothing whatsoever about the relative strength of the contestants (she has not even heard their names before) and she has no other information that is relevant for predicting the winner of the match. Match C is similar to match B, except that Miss Julie has happened to hear that one of the contestants is an excellent tennis player, although she does not know anything about which player it is, and the second player is indeed an amateur so that everybody considers the outcome of the match a foregone conclusion.

Gärdenfors and Sahlin (1982)

Thus, we have an additional source of information for the assessment of each probability. This addition is easiest expressed as the width of the probability interval, where a more narrow interval stands for the decision-maker being more sure of the probability of the event, not more certain of the event itself occurring. This is an important distinction, highlighted in the next example.

Example 4.1: The task is to assign numbers to the following three sentences regarding the probability of an event that has yet to occur:

- "I do not have a clue."
- "I think it is around fifty-fifty."
- "I'm sure it is exactly 50%."

While standard probability theory is forced to assign the probability of 50% in all three cases, interval-probability theory assigns varying amounts of basic probability to the event E and leaves the rest unassigned. With interval probabilities, the first sentence might be translated into the interval [0%, 100%], the second one into [40%, 60%], and the last one into a precise number, i.e. an interval [50%, 50%], respectively.

An approach similar to Walley's was taken by Arthur Dempster already in 1967, where he suggested a way of modelling upper and lower probabilities. This was further developed by his student Glenn Shafer in 1976 when he introduced the concept of basic probability assignments. Within the field of artificial intelligence, the Dempster-Shafer theory for quantifying subjective judgments has received a lot of attention, but it has been deemed to be unnecessarily strong with respect to interval representation by Kurt Weichselberger and Sigrid Pöhlmann in 1990. Weichselberger's theory of interval-probability argues in favour of a system for interval probabilities clearly related to the one of Kolmogorov, in his own words:

> Altogether, a theory of interval-probability comes nearer to the classical understanding of probability assignment than those approaches relying on more general types of assessment.
>
> **Weichselberger (1999)**

Fuzzy set theory, first suggested by Lotfi Zadeh in 1965, should also be mentioned as a widespread approach to relaxing the requirement of numerically precise data and providing a more realistic model of the vagueness in subjective estimates of probabilities and values. This approach allows, among other features, the decision-maker to model and evaluate a decision situation in vague linguistic terms and introduce various (often rather complicated) rules for aggregating this information. Similarly, possibility theory was introduced, in connection with fuzzy set theory, to allow reasoning with imprecise or vague knowledge. The measures defined are usually local over simple sets, and it is often hard to obtain an intuitive understanding of the global meaning of various combinations of them. Furthermore, fuzzy approaches are restricted in the sense that they do not really handle qualitative aspects such as comparisons between different components in many decision situations. One major disadvantage of such formalisms is the problem of communication between analysts and stakeholders. While sometimes possessing attractive mathematical properties, the basic concepts are most often not known to the decision-makers and thus feel unfamiliar, creating a knowledge gap hard to bridge.

In contrast to both Dempster-Shafer theory and fuzzy theory, traditional interval decision analysis conforms to statistical reasoning by being compatible with the concept of admissibility which we will explore in Chapter 5. The emphasis is not on establishing another formalism for representing imprecision but rather on presenting a way of handling the imprecision inherent in many real-life decision problems within standard decision analysis. Moreover, the possibility to state, e.g., that one consequence is inferior to another is very useful, particularly when handling qualitative information. Therefore, in addition to allowing interval statements, some modern decision methods allow statements containing comparisons between probabilities or between values.

The same question that troubles probability statements applies to value (or utility) statements as well. What if the decision-maker does not know any exact value for a particular consequence? In that case, it would be desirable to be able to use statements such as "the monetary value of consequence C is between $25,000 and $40,000 or the value of consequence C is between 30 and 50." Traditional methods from utility theory do not allow for this. They again require precise numerical values, no matter how unsure the decision-maker is, and so do not offer an opportunity to express any degree of uncertainty. Next, we will look at how to utilise imprecise information in a real-life decision process.

4.2 A Decision Process

The remainder of this chapter is divided into three sections. The first section describes a decision work process that uses an imprecise interval method. The second section presents a decision problem on which a sample decision session in the last section is built. The purpose is not to describe the mathematical or computational machinery necessary but rather to give an intuitive feeling for how an interval method works and for its relevance to decision-making. Another objective is to demonstrate that the suggested method is realistic to work with.

A feature of the method is that the decision-maker has to make his or her problem statements more visible than he or she would otherwise. This brings about a number of advantages. First, he or she must make the underlying information clear, and second, the statements can be the subject of discussions with (and criticism from) other possible participants in the decision process. Third, it can also be seen more clearly which information is required in order to "solve" the problem and within which areas some more information must be gathered before a well-founded decision can be made. Fourth, arguments for (and against) a specific choice can be derived from the analysis material. Fifth, the decision can be better documented, and the underlying information as well as the reasoning leading up to a decision can be traced afterward. The decision can even be changed in a controlled way, should new information become available at a later stage.

Decision-makers in private as well as in business situations often use rather simple decision models to aid decisions. In many cases, decisions are made without employing any model at all. The decision might be based on rules of thumb or on intuition, or even be a repetition of a similar decision made earlier. Sometimes, decisions are made after listing the alternatives and discussing their consequences in an unstructured manner. Recall that they state the advantages and disadvantages of each course of action. When the special case of one action having all advantages and another all disadvantages does not prevail, it is necessary to make a comparison between the consequences of all alternatives. Examples of more structured decision aids include decision matrices and decision trees as discussed in previous chapters. One possible disadvantage is that either they do not handle probabilities at all (matrices) or they require the decision-maker to make probability statements with precise numeric values, however unsure he or she is of his or her estimates. Whether this is a real disadvantage is discussed in Chapter 8 on guidelines for selecting decision methods specifically for each situation.

Suppose a decision-maker wants to evaluate a specific decision situation in a structured way. In order to solve the problem, given available resources, a decision process such as the following is suggested.

- Clarify the problem; divide it into sub-problems if necessary
- Decide which information is a prerequisite for the decision
- Collect and compile the information
- Define possible courses of action
- For each alternative:
  - Identify possible consequences
  - For each consequence:
    - If possible, estimate how probable it is
    - If possible, estimate the value if it occurs
- Disregard obviously bad courses of action
- Based on the above, evaluate the remaining alternatives
- Carry out a sensitivity analysis
- Choose a "reasonable" alternative

The model described in the following should be seen in the context of such a decision process.

The decision process is carried out in a number of steps presented here in work-cycle form. A work cycle consists of six phases (Figure 4.1). The first step of the first cycle is special since there is often much initial information to collect.

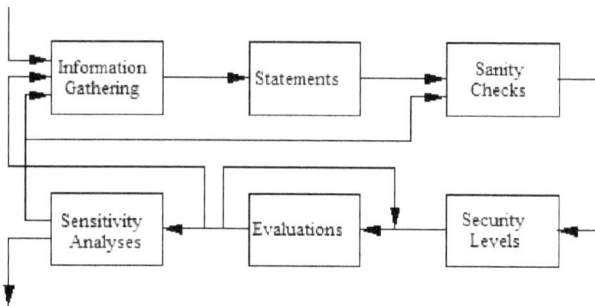

Figure 4.1 A work cycle.

The initial information is gathered from different sources. Then, it is formulated in statements. Following that, an iterative process commences where step by step the decision-maker gains further insights and sometimes a conclusion. During this process, the decision-maker receives help in realising which information is missing, too vague, or too precise. He or she might also change the problem structure by adding or removing consequences or even entire alternatives as more decision information becomes available.

4.2.1 Information Gathering

In some cases, the first information collection phase can be a rather long step. In a business setting with larger investigations, it might take months and result in documentation covering a large shelf space. In other cases, it might only require a few half-day discussions or less. It is impossible to describe any typical case because the situations are too diverse.

After the data collection phase, a filtering task commences where the decision-maker structures and orders the information. He or she tries to compile a smaller number of reasonable courses of action and identify the consequences belonging to each alternative. There is no requirement for the alternatives to contain the same number of consequences. However, within any given alternative, it is required that the consequences are exclusive and exhaustive, i.e. whatever the result, it should be covered by the description of exactly one consequence. This is unproblematic since a residual consequence can be added to take care of unspecified events.

4.2.2 Statements

Once the information is structured, it is formulated in the form of interval statements such as "the probability of consequence C occurring is less than 40%." Intervals are a natural form in which to express such imprecise statements. It is not required that the consequence sets are fixed from the outset. A new consequence may be added at a later stage, thus facilitating an incremental style of working.

Likewise, the values can be expressed as interval statements. When all statements in the current cycle have been made, the data collection phase is almost over. As the insights into the decision problem accumulate during all the following phases, add new information and alter or delete information already entered.

4.2.3 Sanity Checks

Thereafter, the work cycle goes into finishing the data collection. In this step, the sanity of the information is checked. There is always a risk of the collected information being cluttered or misunderstood. Descriptive decision theory lists many biases and fallacies that a decision-maker could be subject to. As we saw in Chapter 3, these include heuristics of availability, bandwagon effects, information cascades, base rate fallacies, probability neglects, exaggerated expectations, framing, and groupthink in general. It is nearly impossible, though, for a normal decision-maker to be on the lookout for all of these, and thus a more general approach is required. The three best general countermeasures against biases and fallacies are a) sample several information sources if possible, b) revisit the information sources several times, and c) ask others for their assessments of your information and how you have interpreted it.

4.2.4 Security Levels

Many decisions are one-off decisions or are important enough not to allow a too undesirable outcome regardless of it having a very low probability. The principle of maximising the expected value (PMEV) decision rule will not rule out an alternative with such a consequence, provided it has a low probability. If the probability for a very undesirable consequence is larger than some security level, it seems reasonable to require that the alternative should not be considered, regardless of whether the expected value shows it to be a good course of action. If the security level is violated by one or more consequences in an alternative, then the alternative is deemed unsafe and should be disregarded. An example of security levelling is an insurance company desiring not to enter into insurance agreements where the profitability is high but there is a very small but not negligible risk for the outcome to be a loss large enough to put the company's existence at stake. As we saw in Chapter 3, security levels are an important supplement to the PMEV.

4.2.5 Evaluations

After having taken security levels into account, which value does a particular decision have? In cases where the outcomes can be assigned monetary values, it seems natural that the value of the decision should be some kind of aggregation of the values of the individual consequences. The prevalent suggestion is to assign different weights to the consequences so that more probable ones are more influential than less probable ones. As we saw in the previous chapter, this line of reasoning leads to the expected value and the PMEV rule.

The next question is how to compare the courses of action using this rule when probabilities and values are stated in the form of intervals. This is not a trivial task, since usually, the possible expected values of alternatives overlap. The most favourable assignments of numbers to variables for an alternative usually render that alternative the preferred one. The first step towards a usable decision rule is to establish some concepts that tell when one alternative is preferable to another. For simplicity, only two alternatives are discussed, but the reasoning can easily be generalised to any number of alternatives. Let the expected value of an alternative A be denoted $E(A)$.

- Alternative A_1 is *at least as good as* A_2 if $E(A_1) \geq E(A_2)$ for all combinations of probability and value variables.
- Alternative A_1 is *better than* A_2 if it is at least as good as A_2 and further $E(A_1) > E(A_2)$ for some combination of probability and value variables.
- An alternative is *admissible* if no other alternative is better.

If there is only one admissible alternative, it is obviously the preferred choice. Usually, there is more than one since apparently good or bad alternatives are normally dealt with on a manual basis before structured decision methods are brought into use. All non-admissible alternatives should be removed from the considered ones and should not take a further part in the evaluation. The existence of more than one admissible alternative means that for different consistent assignments of numbers to the probability and value variables, different courses of action are preferable. When this occurs, how is it possible to find out which alternative to prefer? In the ensuing example, we will look at that.

4.2.6 Sensitivity Analyses

After the evaluation, a sensitivity analysis is the next step. The analysis tries to show what parts of the given information are most critical for the obtained results and must therefore be given extra careful consideration. This is accomplished by varying a number of statements in desired ways, increasing or decreasing intervals, modifying structural information, etc. It also points to which information is too vague to be of any assistance to the ongoing evaluation. Information identified in this way is subject to reconsideration, thereby triggering a new work cycle. In the case of using a software decision tool (recommended), this is taken care of automatically.

Before a new cycle starts, alternatives found to be undesirable or obviously inferior from new information arriving are removed from the decision process. Likewise, a new alternative can be added, should the information gathered indicate the need for it. Consequences in an alternative can be added or removed as necessary to reflect changes in the model. Often a number of cycles are necessary to produce an interesting and reliable result.

4.2.7 Decision Process Results

After a number of work cycles have been completed, both the decision problem and its proposed solution(s) in the form of preferred courses of action will be fairly well documented especially for decisions in business settings. Anyone interested and with access to the information can afterward check and verify (and criticise) the decision based on the output documentation, which, because all consequences are clearly presented, shows how all the alternative courses of action have been valued. Also, during the decision process, the analysis is open for comments and can become the basis for further discussions. Another effect is that the decisions are less dependent on which employee handles a particular decision situation since deviations from the corporate policy can be detected in the documentation after the process has been completed if not earlier.

4.3 A Decision Example

This section presents an example of a decision problem suitable for investigation using an interval method. A medium-sized manufacturing company relied, in one of its most important production lines, on an old machine for which spare parts had become increasingly harder to obtain. At a critical moment, the machine broke down in a more serious way than previously. It became clear to management that the machine was a potential threat to future operations unless it was either thoroughly repaired or replaced by a new machine.

Scanning the market for this type of machine, the production engineers found that such machines are no longer on the market in the Western world. Newer, multi-purpose machines have taken their places but at markedly higher investment costs. In some of the newly industrialised countries (NICs), though, those older single-purpose machines are still a popular choice for their relative cheapness and durability, especially in places with little access to preventive maintenance. Thus, management is faced with the following decision situation involving three alternatives:

- A_1 – *repair the old machine*: This would be possible with custom-made spare parts but at higher costs and with unknown quality. Also, the future capacity of the machine is doubtful as many other parts of it are approaching the age limit.
- A_2 – *purchase a similar machine from a NIC country*: There are a number of suppliers to choose from, but they are all located far away from Sweden, and the representatives in Europe are not familiar with selling this kind of equipment, thus making the supply of service hard to predict.
- A_3 – *purchase a modern machine*: Such machines are available from several suppliers in Europe. Their representatives in Sweden are used to selling this kind of equipment, thus making the possession of the machine quite uncomplicated. A modern machine, though, has many more functions than required for the job, and the cost of the extra features drains the cash flow from the production line.

When selecting a particular course of action, a number of consequences may occur during the five-year write-off period considered. It is important that for each action, the set of consequences in the method is exhaustive and exclusive, i.e. exactly one consequence will subsequently occur. For the three alternatives, the following consequences were identified.

Alternative A_1 – repairing the old machine:

- C_1: The machine will be out of order for a considerable part of the next five years and will not function properly when in operation. The result is both less quantity and less quality than today and than the customers expect.
- C_2: The machine will be working most of the time but will not function properly when in operation. The result is full quantity but less quality than today and than the customers expect.
- C_3: The machine will be working most of the time and will function properly when in operation, almost as it did before the major breakdown. The result is the full quantity and full quality as the customers expect.

Alternative A_2 – purchasing a similar machine from a NIC country:

- C_4: The new machine will be working most of the time but will not function properly when in operation. The result is full quantity but less quality than today and than the customers expect.
- C_5: The new machine will be working most of the time and will function properly when in operation, almost as the old machine did before the major breakdown. The result is full quantity and full quality as the customers expect.

Alternative A_3 – purchasing a modern machine from a local supplier:

- C_6: The modern machine will be working most of the time and will function properly when in operation, better than the old machine did before the major breakdown. The result is the full quantity and full quality as the customers expect.
- C_7: The modern machine will be working as in C_6. In addition, it admits the production of new goods for which there is a sizeable market. Profits are not that high, though, since the company does not have a strong market position.
- C_8: The modern machine will be working as in C_6. In addition, it admits the production of new goods for which there is a sizeable market. Profits are fairly high since the company does have a leading position in the market.

Table 4.1   Profits

ALTERNATIVE A_1	
Consequence C_1	20–40 MUSD
Consequence C_2	35–50 MUSD
Consequence C_3	50–60 MUSD
ALTERNATIVE A_2	
Consequence C_4	35–50 MUSD
Consequence C_5	50–60 MUSD
ALTERNATIVE A_3	
Consequence C_6	50–60 MUSD
Consequence C_7	60–80 MUSD
Consequence C_8	70–100 MUSD

The profits over the five-year period when adopting the alternatives of the respective alternatives have been estimated by the financial department. They are given as ranges and are shown in Table 4.1. The costs of adopting the alternatives of the respective alternatives have also been estimated by the staff. They are given as ranges and are shown in Table 4.2. Note that the greater uncertainty regarding the costs of repairing the old machine is reflected in wider cost intervals.

The net profits over the five-year period are then calculated as profits minus investment costs. They are given as ranges in Table 4.3.

Finally, the probabilities of all consequences within each alternative were estimated, given that the alternative was chosen. They are given as ranges in Table 4.4.

This is the initial specification of the decision problem of the company. Next, it will be entered into a computer tool and analysed. This section uses the computer software DecideIT that is bundled with this, book but any other similar software can be used. The functions of the DecideIT user interface are described in the Appendix.

The problem according to the description above and in Tables 4.3 and 4.4 has been entered into the program. The resulting decision can be seen in Figure 4.2. Now, the analysis of the problem can begin.

Table 4.2   Action Costs

Alternative A_1	5–10 MUSD
Alternative A_2	10–12 MUSD
Alternative A_3	25–30 MUSD

Table 4.3 Net Profits

ALTERNATIVE A_1	
Consequence C_1	10–35 MUSD
Consequence C_2	20–45 MUSD
Consequence C_3	35–55 MUSD
ALTERNATIVE A_2	
Consequence C_4	23–40 MUSD
Consequence C_5	38–50 MUSD
ALTERNATIVE A_3	
Consequence C_6	20–45 MUSD
Consequence C_7	30–55 MUSD
Consequence C_8	40–75 MUSD

The first step is to see if any alternative is too undesirable to be further processed, i.e. if a security level has been violated. Setting the security level to a 10% probability of a value of \$10M or lower yields a 30% belief that the resulting expected value of alternative 1 is below the security level while there are no such risks for alternatives 2 or 3. This shows that alternative 1 is somewhat problematic – with 70% confidence the alternative is not in the risk zone as specified in the analysis (the outcome having a value of \$10 million or less with at least 10% probability). This is not dangerous enough to warrant the exclusion of the alternative but it casts some doubt on it.

Thus, we proceed with a cardinal ranking, showing the possible overlap in expected value between the alternatives.

Now, the alternatives' expected values are shown together with the level of confidence in the results. Figure 4.3 shows the ranking

Table 4.4 Probabilities

ALTERNATIVE A_1	
Consequence C_1	5–25%
Consequence C_2	10–30%
Consequence C_3	45–70%
ALTERNATIVE A_2	
Consequence C_4	25–45%
Consequence C_5	50–80%
ALTERNATIVE A_3	
Consequence C_6	60–80%
Consequence C_7	5–15%
Consequence C_8	5–10%

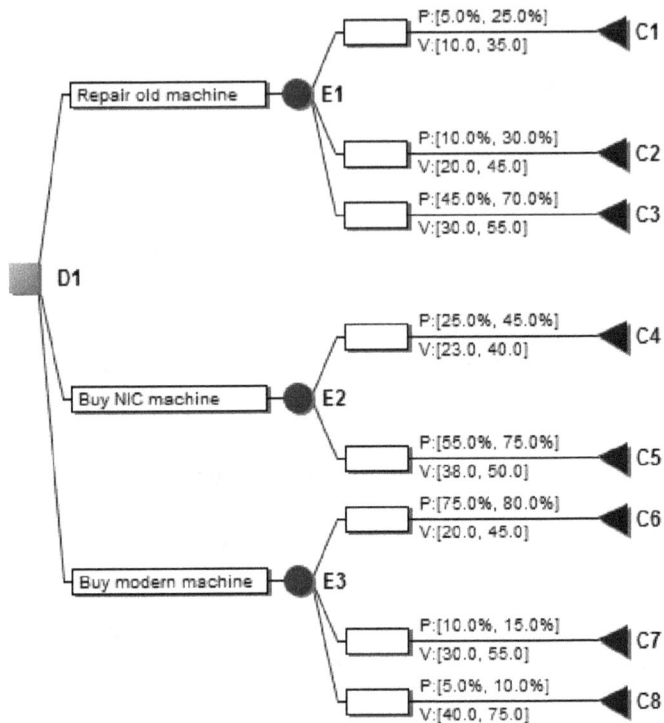

Figure 4.2 The decision tree.

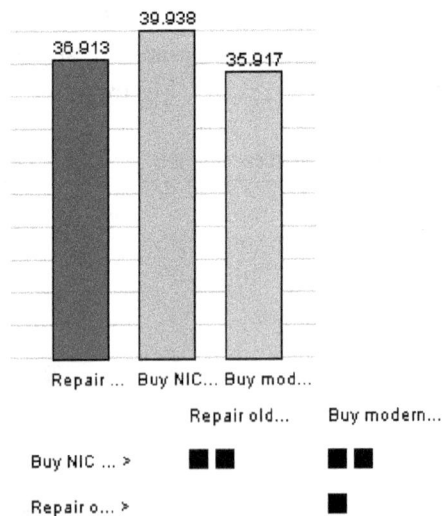

Figure 4.3 Expected values.

2–1–3 among the alternatives. The number of black squares indicates the confidence in the results, with three squares indicating more than 90% confidence and two squares 75–90%. Thus, with at least 75% confidence, alternative 2 is the best one. The highest confidence level is not reached due to the rather wide intervals in the input information. Also, remember that alternative 1 is at doubt already on security grounds earlier. After having considered the evidence for and against the alternatives, alternative 2 is selected as the preferred course of action in this case. A new machine is bought from an NIC country.

5

MULTI-CRITERIA
DECISION-MAKING

There are basically two main branches within modern decision theory: decisions under strict uncertainty and risk (probabilistic or Bayesian decisions), which we have encountered so far in this book, and multi-criteria decisions, which we will discuss in this chapter and in the following chapters. Despite similarities between the branches, these two approaches have separate traditions within which they evolve.

Over the years, the development of decision-making procedures and processes has shifted from a fundamental study of decision theory primarily for single-criteria decisions to a decision-making approach to multi-criteria decisions, often involving conflicting information. In particular, the field of Multi-Criteria Decision Analysis (MCDA) has emerged as a promising discipline that allows for a better understanding of the trade-offs involved in decision-making, such as, between economic, social, and environmental criteria.

Having said this, the same principles that appear in single-criterion decisions reappear in MCDA, so nothing has been wasted by first considering single-criterion decision situations in this book and then moving on to multi-criteria situations. On the contrary, an understanding of the mechanisms governing real-life decision-making under a single criterion makes us very well-equipped to address the case where there is more than one criterion present. Besides, as we will see in Chapter 8, some decision problems can preferably be handled as single-criterion decisions even when they are not.

How should decision-makers compare alternatives based on different decision criteria (objectives)? Already in 1976, Ralph Keeney and Howard Raiffa presented four major real-life decision-making cases in their book *Decisions with Multiple Objectives: Preferences and Value Trade-offs*. In these cases, decision-makers were unable to hide from the conflict between multiple objectives. One example involved the siting of a new airport near

DOI: 10.1201/9781003406709-5

Mexico City, requiring the head of the Department of Public Works to balance objectives such as minimising costs, maximising airport facility capacity, promoting regional development, and minimising visit times for travellers. These large examples made many people see the potential of applying MCDA methods to very large social decision-making problems.

As its name conveys, multi-criteria decisions contain several criteria, sometimes in a hierarchy (tree). There is thus a set of criteria under which the various alternatives are considered. The alternatives are assessed by the decision-maker assigning values to each alternative. The possible consequences (one per alternative under each criterion) are assigned values and then the relative importance of the criteria themselves is represented by weights that can be assigned in different ways which we will discuss below.

The most widely used decision method in MCDA is the additive value rule, sometimes referred to as the weighted sum. In the same manner as for probabilities in the Bayesian case, the weights are restricted by a so-called normalisation constraint, i.e. the weights should sum to 1 (100%). The weighted sum is then the sum of the contributions of each criterion and where each contribution is the product of the criteria weight and the value under that criterion. It is not as complicated as it sounds. For a decision situation with two criteria numbered 1 and 2 (having weights w_1 and w_2, respectively), and with two alternatives A and B where the value of alternative A under criterion 1 is denoted v_{1A} (and v_{2A} under criterion 2), the total weighted value for alternative A is $w_1 \cdot v_{1A} + w_2 \cdot v_{2A}$, and similarly, the weighted value for alternative B can be calculated. Recall that the weights, in this case $w_1 + w_2$, always sum to 1 (100%). Here, the kinship with the expected value for decisions under risk can be seen. Also there, we have the requirement that some entity, in that case probabilities, sum to 1. The difference is that the weights are the same in calculating the weighted value of the different alternatives while for the expected value, the probabilities can differ among the alternatives.

In MCDA, different methods have been proposed by which a decision-maker can express criteria weights. Such methods are sometimes based on scoring points, as in point allocation or direct rating methods. In point allocation, the decision-maker is given a point sum such as 100 to distribute among the criteria. Sometimes, this is pictured as putty with a total mass of 100 being divided into parts and put on the criteria. The more the mass, the larger the weight on that criterion, and thus, the more important it is. When all except one criterion have received their weights, the last criterion's weight is automatically determined as the remaining putty mass. In direct rating, on the other hand, there is no limit to the total number of points to be allocated. The decision-maker allocates as many points as desired to each criterion. The points are subsequently normalised by dividing by the sum of points allocated so that the sum is the same as in the point allocation case. Note that when all but one criterion have received their weights, the last criterion's weight in the direct rating method still has to be explicitly assigned by the decision-maker. Somewhat surprisingly, these two methods of allocating weights yield different results and a reasonable decision method must cater to both ways of handling since we do not know which weighting method a particular decision-maker uses or is perhaps using something in between.

This chapter discusses three types of methods that allow a relaxation of the requirement for precision but keeping with simplicity and without resorting to interval or mixed approaches. Instead, we will here discuss if good decision quality can be obtained without significantly increasing either the elicitational or the computational efforts involved and without making it difficult for a decision-maker to understand the process. The types are:

- Proportional scoring methods
- Ratio scoring methods
- Ranking methods

5.1 Proportional Scoring

One of the most popular proportional scoring methods is the Simple Multi-Attribute Rating Technique (SMART) family of decision analysis methods. Originally introduced by Ward Edwards in 1971, SMART is a seven-step process for creating and analysing decision models. He proposes a method for assessing criteria weights. The criteria are then ranked, and, e.g., 10 points are assigned to the weight of the least important criterion. The other weights are then scored in order of increasing importance according to the decision-maker's preference. In this way, the points represent (somewhat indeterminate) weights. This is thus a direct rating method rather than a point allocation one. The total value of the alternatives is then a weighted average of the values assigned to alternatives under each criterion. In an additive model, weights reflect the importance of one criterion relative to other criteria. But the importance of a criterion largely depends on its generality, which we call weight/scale duality.

Consider for a short moment that you are going to buy a flashlight. You consider three models: A, B, and C, and consider them from two perspectives (criteria): cost and brightness. Of course, you want it to be as cheap as possible but since you will use it quite often at long distances, high brightness leading to a long beam distance is also important. Brightness (measured in lumen) drives production costs, so the most expensive flashlight has the longest beam distance. Now, you need to find a trade-off between the two criteria, i.e. assign weights to them so that their sum is 100%. Note, however, that a statement such as "cost is the most important criterion" is meaningless. Why? Assume that the models have the following costs: A: $70, B: $65, and C: $60, and the following brightnesses: A: 2000 lumen, B: 500 lumen, and C: 200 lumen. Since the difference in cost is so small, it is not in this case very important at all. If instead, we would have had A: $200, B: $100, and C: $50 and A: 1,000 lumen, B: 900 lumen, and C: 800 lumen, then surely cost would have been the decisive criterion. Thus, the weights for the criteria cannot be set as if they were freestanding entities, but they must always be set relative to the difference between the best and the worst alternative for each criterion. This is called the weight/scale-dualism and is a common mistake that decision-makers do. We will discuss it in Chapter 6 on the Pilot Method.

This weight/scale-dualism is one reason why methods like the original SMART, which do not consider the dualism specifically, have been criticised. As a result, the SMART method was subsequently amended with a swing technique (and renamed SMARTS), addressing the criticism by changing the weight elicitation procedure. Basically, swing works like this:

- Select a scale, e.g. positive integers
- Consider the difference between the worst and the best alternatives within each criterion
- Imagine a fictitious alternative (called the zero alternative) with the worst alternatives from the respective criteria,

- For each criterion in turn, consider the improvement (swing) in the zero alternative by having the worst alternative in that criterion replaced by the best one
- Assign numbers (importance) to each criterion in such a way that they correspond to the assessed improvement from having the criterion changed from the worst to the best alternative

In this way, weights are assigned with the desired property that they are relative, i.e. the weights reflect the underlying values in each alternative. However, this procedure can be perceived as a bit complicated, and a similar but simpler way of handling this issue is presented in Chapter 6 on the Pilot Method.

5.2 Ratio Scoring

One of the most well-known ratio-scoring methods is the Analytic Hierarchy Process (AHP) suggested by Thomas Saaty in 1977. The basic idea in AHP is to assess a set of decision alternatives by pairwise comparisons. For each criterion, the decision-maker should first find the ordering of the alternatives from best to worst. Next, he or she should find the strength of the ordering by considering pairwise ratios (pairwise relations) between the alternatives using the integers 1, 3, 5, 7, and 9 to express their relative strengths, indicating that one alternative is equally good as another (strength = 1) or three, five, seven, or nine times as good. But exactly what, e.g., "seven times as good" actually means is sometimes hard to determine, leading to a risk for less reliable assessment between decision-makers as well as for the same decision-maker on different occasions. Furthermore, the AHP method is cognitively demanding in practice due to the large number of pairwise comparisons required as the number of criteria increases. This is why ratios are not included in the Pilot Method.

5.3 Ranking

It often turns out that rankings are easier to provide than precise numbers, and for that reason, various criteria weight techniques have been developed based on rankings. One influential idea is to derive so-called surrogate weights from rankings. The resulting ranking is converted into numerical weights, and it is important to do this with as small an information loss as possible while still preserving the correctness of the weight assignments. William Stillwell, David Seaver, and Ward Edwards introduced weight approximation techniques already in 1981 in the form of the so-called rank sum and rank reciprocal weights. A decade later, Hutton Barron and Bruce Barrett (1996) suggested another, mathematically more advanced weight method, the rank order centroid (ROC) weights that had some good properties but was felt to favour the highest ranked criterion a bit too much.

In the decades following, more surrogate weights were suggested and their performances were thoroughly compared, not least by the authors of this book. Most of these surrogates have a more complicated mathematical form and are best used in computer programs for decision analysis. From our research, a clear winner for manual, pen-and-paper, decision methods has emerged. The rank sum method stands out as the primary candidate for manual procedures and is hence included in the Pilot Method in Chapter 6.

5.4 Other Approaches

Other approaches to decision evaluation under multiple objectives include the outranking methods Preference Ranking Organization Method for Enrichment of Evaluations (PROMETHEE) of Jean-Pierre Brans, Bertrand Mareschal, and Philippe Vincke (1984) and ÉLimination Et Choix Traduisant la REalité (ELECTRE) of Bernard Roy (1991) and Philippe Vincke (1992). These methods are based on a partial ordering of the alternatives and are often referred to as the French school of decision aids. ELECTRE is based on a search for outranking relations deduced from a set of binary preference relations. In that context, Jean Simos proposed a simple procedure, using a set of cards, trying to indirectly determine numerical values for criteria weights. The Simos method is a bit different from the methods discussed above. It is a relatively simple way to handle relations between criteria, introducing cardinality if necessary. Using this method, one or a group of decision-makers are given a set of coloured cards with criteria names. Additionally, the decision-maker(s) receive a set of white (blank) cards. After that, they are supposed to rank the non-blank cards from least important to most important, putting criteria of perceived equal importance in the same position. Additionally, decision-makers are asked to place white cards between coloured cards to express preference strength. Then, the surrogate numbers can be calculated according to the Simos procedure.

One problem with Simos' method is that it is not robust when preferences change and thus has some other counterintuitive properties. Because the weights are determined differently depending on the number of cards in the subsets of equally ranked cards, the differences between the weights also change in an uncontrolled way when the cards are reordered. This is the reason why a revised Simos procedure was suggested where a more robust behaviour when using these white cards was provided. This was accomplished by requesting the decision-makers to state how many times more important the most important criterion is compared to the least important, somewhat in the fashion of the AHP method above. Such multiplicative statements have proven harder to make than simpler comparisons on which criterion is more or less important (ordinal rankings). So while this addition seemingly solves one problem, it also introduces the complication to require the decision-maker to reliably and correctly estimate a proportional (multiplicative) factor between the largest and the smallest criteria weights. This further complicates the method and increases the risk of making mistakes in modelling. For those reasons, while the Simos method is elegant and useful, it is not considered or included in neither the Rank Three procedure presented in the next section nor the Pilot Method presented in Chapter 6.

5.5 Rank Three

Rank Three is a decision procedure that uses ranking as discussed in this chapter. It is particularly well suited to quick multi-criteria decision-making, also in groups when there are more than one decision-maker with equal say. To begin with, establish which alternatives there are to choose from in your decision situation. If a group is involved, make sure everyone in the group agrees on the alternatives and what they entail, i.e. the consequences if they are chosen. Next, establish which criteria (perspectives) the alternatives should be assessed under. Again, if you are in a group, make sure everyone understands the criteria in the same way.

Once you have your criteria, the next step is to assess the alternatives under each criterion in turn. You make the assessment by ranking the three best alternatives under a criterion so that the best receives 3 points, the second best 2 points, and the third best 1 point. All the other alternatives score no points at all, but the worst alternative is marked with an asterisk. Ties are allowed, i.e. more than one alternative can be deemed to belong to, e.g., the second best category and then they receive 2 points each. If this is a group decision, each member of the group does this ranking individually.

Following the assessment of the alternatives, next turn to the criteria. When ranking the criteria, it is very important to consider the differences between the best and the worst alternatives within each criterion. Recall the flashlight example earlier in this chapter. To prepare for ranking, assume that you have eight alternatives named A–H and that for the first criterion, you have given 3 points to alternative C and put the asterisk on alternative G. Then you write "Alternative G → Alternative C" next to that criterion to remind you of which alternatives are the worst and best within the criterion and proceed to do the same for all criteria. Rank the criteria so that the most important one receives 3 points, the second most important 2 points, and all the other ones 1 point. Again, ties are allowed, so if more than one criterion is seen as, e.g., most important, then they receive 3 points each. No criterion gets 0 points as opposed to the ranking of alternatives.

To arrive at a decision, calculate the total score for the alternatives one by one. This is done in two steps. In the first step, for the criterion with 3 points, multiply the alternatives' point scores by 3, and for the criterion with 2 points, multiply the alternatives' point scores by 2. In the second step, sum up all the points for each alternative to obtain their final scores. The alternative with the highest score is the preferred alternative.

Example 5.1: Assume that you are a policymaker who is in charge of issuing a policy for reduced food waste in your hometown. You have six alternatives: 1. mandatory recycling, 2. voluntary food-sharing initiatives, 3. increased sales tax on food, 4. restrained opening hours in grocery stores, 5. Increased expiry date recommendations, and 6. large information campaigns. It has been decided that you

Table 5.1 Ranking of Alternatives and Criteria Importance

WEIGHTS	2 FEASIBILITY	1 IMPACT	3 ECONOMICS	1 POLITICS	1 SPEED
ALTERNATIVE 1	3		1	2	3
ALTERNATIVE 2		*	3	1	2
ALTERNATIVE 3		2	2	*	
ALTERNATIVE 4	2				
ALTERNATIVE 5	1	1	1	3	1
ALTERNATIVE 6	*	3	*		*

should assess these alternatives under five criteria: feasibility, impact, economics, politics, and speed of implementation.

For each criterion, you rank the three best alternatives and mark the worst with an asterisk. Next, you rank the criteria by comparing their respective importance by comparing each criterion's difference between the worst and the best alternative, i.e. that with an asterisk and that with 3 points. Note the tie for third place (1 point) under the criterion Economics. Then you arrive at the decision (Table 5.1).

To obtain the final ranking of the alternatives, you multiply the columns that have weights 3 and 2 with those numbers and sum up each row to the total in the right column in Table 5.2.

The higher the sum, the better ranking for that alternative. So in this example, information campaigns is the preferred alternative followed by voluntary food-sharing.

If this were a group decision to be made, there is one more step. Each participant gives 3 points to his or her highest scoring alternative and 2 and 1 point, respectively, to the second and third highest. This time, ties are *not* allowed since that would increase the influence

Table 5.2 Result of the Rank Three Procedure

WEIGHTS	2 FEASIBILITY	1 IMPACT	3 ECONOMICS	1 POLITICS	1 SPEED	TOTAL
ALTERNATIVE 1	6		3	2	3	14
ALTERNATIVE 2			9	1	2	12
ALTERNATIVE 3		2	6			8
ALTERNATIVE 4	4					4
ALTERNATIVE 5	2	1	3	3	1	10
ALTERNATIVE 6		3				3

of that participant. Instead, a participant with alternatives tied at the same sum has to choose which one of these alternatives is ranked the highest. This concludes the description of Rank Three, which is a very lightweight method with reasonable precision. For more complex decisions or if higher precision is desired, turn to the Pilot Method which is a very powerful method. But with decision power also comes a somewhat more complex process.

6

THE PILOT METHOD

While decision-making by ranking as described in Chapter 5 can be performed by a software tool such as DecideIT (see the Appendix), in this chapter we will take a look at how easily decisions can also be made using only pen and paper by following the Pilot Method. It is a more thorough and precise method than Rank Three from the previous chapter. Pilot is not an acronym but refers to you being in the pilot's seat when making real-life decisions if you follow the method. The method is the result of many years of research and validation. It is based on observations on what kind of information people can easily provide and handle with reasonably preserved quality. As such, the method does not rely on unrealistic assumptions about decision-makers' time and resources to achieve impeccable decisions. The Pilot Method allows you to sit in the driver's seat when you are going to make decisions that require reflection, either alone or as part of a group. In other words, you become your own decision pilot with the ability to control decision situations without too much risk of making mistakes.

The Pilot Method consists of five decision stages that we will now look into. We will avail ourselves of a worked example to illustrate the stages. The example comes from a personal decision, but this does not mean that the Pilot approach is any less suited to decisions for businesses or organisations than to personal decisions. Not at all. The example was chosen so that most readers can recognise themselves and be able to easily relate to the different decision stages. Note that the terms *alternative* and *option* will be used interchangeably in this chapter to lighten up the text – they refer to the same thing.

The method comes in two versions comprising four and five stages, respectively. The four-stage method (PM4) considers the cost aspect from the very start of the process while the five-stage method (PM5) focuses on functionality in the first four stages and devotes the fifth stage entirely to the cost aspect. If there is no cost aspect involved in the decision, the versions are identical. The first three or four stages

DOI: 10.1201/9781003406709-6
63

of the method ensure that we gradually work our way towards better and better decision information in terms of the features and functions of our options for action. And the last stage makes a final evaluation of our information base. At each stage, our information base gains in quality. But already after the first stage, we will have a fully operational decision-making basis, and for some decisions, we might decide to make do with that. Time is money, and there are many decision situations where the most preferable option becomes clear quite early in this process. In that case, there is really no need to continue with any more stages or analyses. The Pilot Method is divided into the following stages:

1. First, we create a so-called pro and contra list (P-C list) for each alternative. Such a list includes the advantages and disadvantages we can see. We might already make our decision at this point.
2. Otherwise, we record the really important characteristics of the possible options in the decision situation. Perhaps this is enough for making our decision.
3. Else we rank all the options under each criterion separately. This will give us a really good basis for our decision.
4. If we continue, then we assign weights to the criteria according to a ranking order. In PM4, we are now ready for our final decision while in PM5 we are almost there.
5. In PM5 only, the fifth stage manages the trade-off between cost versus functionality and features of our available options.

Why two versions of the method? There are two distinct types of decision situations. On the one hand, there are decisions where we choose between alternative courses of action either mostly based on their functional properties or where cost is a perspective among others, albeit often the highest ranked criterion. For these decisions, using PM4 the outcome (decision) is settled at the latest after the fourth stage, or earlier after as many stages as we see the need to complete. On the other hand, there are decisions that primarily focus on the most cost-effective option, which is often not the option with the best functional properties but rather combines reasonably good properties with a low cost. Using PM5, the fifth stage is separate and necessary for this type of decision in order to find the most cost-effective option, no matter how many of the previous four stages we carry out to rank the options functionally. As examples of the latter type of decision, procurements come to mind.

There are two equally important effects of a decision analysis using the Pilot Method. The first is reaching clear and, as far as possible, accurate results from the completed procedure. The results give a good indication of which decision you should make, but we should always bear in mind that decision analysis is the basis for the decision and that the real decision is always made by a human decision-maker. The second effect, which is just as important, is the increased awareness and understanding of the options as well as of the entire context for the decision, which is achieved by illuminating the decision problem. Options are what we consider choosing between, i.e. what we are going to do. The second parameter is what we consider important, i.e. our criteria for choosing. These must be clear and understandable. The effects of these insights are important, not least when a group should take a decision or when investigators prepare a basis for a decision that needs to be communicated to policymakers or to a management team.

6.1 Stage 1 – P-C Lists

So, how should we approach a decision problem? The first stage is to find out which options are available. Sometimes it is relatively easy to list these, but sometimes they are harder to identify. In many cases, the creation of a process similar to brainstorming is favoured in which creative options of action are produced without the restriction that they must be guaranteed to be realistically feasible. In other cases, there are numerous possible options but it is rarely advisable to have more than ten in an analysis. With many more options, it is best to divide the analysis into two phases. In the first phase, some representative and particularly attractive options are included for each type or cluster of options. When the first phase is completed, the analysis will indicate one or two types that are the most attractive. Then in the second phase, a greater number of options from these preferred types can be included in a more refined analysis. If you really cannot contrive such a division, then there is no formal reason not to include a large number of options in an analysis with only one phase, but in practice, it might become cumbersome.

In this chapter, we will follow Lilly and Larry. They live with their son, Fido, and their dog, Smilla, in a small apartment in the town centre. Fido is soon to start school and needs his own room. For some time, the family has been thinking about moving away from the centre to a larger apartment in a suburb. But there are many suburbs and the choice is not easy. Lilly and Larry have looked at about fifty apartments in the past year but have not been able to decide, and now the start of the school year is approaching rapidly. Above all, buying a larger apartment not only seems both expensive and a bit scary but also seems difficult because there is such a huge selection available and the market is so capricious and nothing quite feels like value for money. They decide to use the Pilot Method to determine which apartment to buy.

They begin with Stage 1, by writing down the apartments they have looked at and liked for whatever reason. It turns into a rather long and confounding list, but when they group them by residential, or rather the type of, area, a pattern emerges. After some contemplation, they have identified eight apartments that well characterise what they have looked at during the past year. They write each apartment's address on a piece of paper and begin writing arguments for and against each apartment. The paper is quickly filled with comments like "great floor plan," "afternoon sun," "feels cramped," "close to school," and "graffiti by entrance gate." But by grouping those into arguments for and against, Lilly and Larry soon see that two of the apartments are out of the question. One is simply too expensive even if it looks great with a terrace and designer kitchen, and the other is so far away that commuting would take unreasonably long. The addresses of the remaining six apartments are A-street No. 1, B-alley No. 2, C-road No. 3, D-crescent No. 4, E-avenue No. 5, and F-square No. 6. The first three seem to be the best at a first glance, but they want to continue with Stage 2 of the method with all six options without trying to decide yet. Parts of the lists from the analysis of the first three options are shown in Table 6.1. The other options are dealt with similarly.

This procedure can be described more generally. Let us assume that there is a set of lists with an easily manageable number of options, maybe five to ten. For each option, we need to develop a so-called P-C list. This list includes the advantages and disadvantages we see in each option. The lists might become relatively long, and the same aspect need not be present on all the lists. When

Table 6.1 The Output of Stage 1 of the Pilot Method Showing the Three First Options

A-STREET NO.1	B-ALLEY NO.2	C-ROAD NO.3	...
Pros:	Pros:	Pros:	...
Cosy living room	Fantastic terrace	Charming block	
Fido has more space	Own study	Good restaurants	
Super & small school	...	...	
...			
Contras:	Contras:	Contras:	...
Rather run-down area	Big anonymous school	Cramped room for Fido	
Far from town but fast	Far from town and slow	Small balcony facing north	
access	access	...	
...	...		

the lists are complete, they are inspected for unacceptable draw-backs. An option with any drawback you cannot live with is rejected no matter how attractive other features of that option may be. Mark all such options and eliminate them from the continuation of the method. This is the security level mechanism from Chapter 3 applied to multi-criteria decision-making. We now have a possibly purged set of lists of options that we could accept as a good decision basis. If we intend to continue with the next stage in the Pilot model, we are now finished with Stage 1.

6.2 Finishing after Stage 1

But if we do not want to continue with more stages and rather want to try to make a decision already now, one finishing step remains which is to inspect the P-C lists. Sort the pros and cons for each option. Lay out the P-C lists with all the options in front of you and weigh the advantages against the disadvantages of the various options. Try to find options that are completely worse than at least one other and eliminate them immediately. If you also find any options that are worse than doing nothing, then eliminate all of these too. Continue this process until you have only two options left. Now is the time to take a break, and when you return, try to convince yourself (or your group if this is a group decision) that this particular option should be selected. The option of the two that prevails by your line of reasoning is the option you should choose from Stage 1. We have now completed the first analysis. If you think that this is sufficient, you need not continue with Stage 2 or any of the other stages (except Stage 5 if you are using PM5). For example, suppose a large terrace was crucial for Lilly and Larry, but they do not care much about the school, then they select option 2, the apartment at B-alley No. 2.

You might think that this is a bit rough and ready, and if you find this last part of Stage 1 to be relatively difficult, that is because it often is. It is precisely for this reason that there are four more stages in the Pilot Method, stages that help you find the best option in your decision-making situation. But sometimes Stage 1 suffices.

6.3 Stage 2 – An Argument Matrix

In Stage 1, we produced a set of options and a P-C list with pros and cons for each of these options. We also ensured that no options with unacceptable characteristics remained.

In Stage 2, it is time to start thinking about values. Which properties of the possible options are really important in this decision situation? Which perspectives on these options are the most important? These perspectives should be grouped together under a number of criteria, where each criterion represents any kind of focus on one or more important perspectives on the decision. The P-C lists from the previous stage are often of great help in finding these criteria. It would be strange if the pros and cons of the options did not relate to what we consider to be essential properties of the criteria we will use to make our decision.

Our example again (Stage 2): Lilly and Larry now have six apartments left, each on its own piece of paper listing its respective pros and cons. In Stage 2, it is now time to think about and decide which features and characteristics (i.e. criteria) are the most important to their decision. Lilly and Larry begin by writing these down in an unsorted list. The list is growing rapidly: "cosy neighbourhood," "many cafes," "lake view," "good school for Fido," "open floor plan," "balcony facing south," "good state of repair," "close to work," "neat indoors," "easy to park," and so on. It soon becomes unmanageable, and Lilly and Larry try to group the desired characteristics into four main groups and one residual group of miscellany. They find this a little bit tricky, but it also affords clarity to the process to have a grouping as a goal. After some thought, they arrive at the following groupings: Area/Location, Planning/Indoor comfort, School,

Commuting/Accessibility, and Miscellaneous. Both Larry and Lilly agree that they think these criteria embrace the most important aspects of the decision situation while some less important ones need to go into the Miscellaneous category. Further, they feel that this order between the criteria corresponds well to how important they perceive their respective criteria to be. Fido is also allowed to have his say too, but mostly so that he feels included.

The next task for Lilly and Larry is to draw up a matrix (table) with the options (apartments) as rows and characteristics (groups of criteria) as columns. They then fill the boxes with text by picking pros and cons from the P-C lists. Most of the boxes get filled, but after they have gone through and checked off all the lists, a few empty boxes remain. The last thing they do in this stage is therefore to complete the empty boxes by filling in their value assessments there too. Feeling quite satisfied, Lilly and Larry look at the matrix (which is partially shown in Table 6.2) to make sure they agree with its contents. They feel they have acquired a much better, overview and structure for their decision. They also feel that this could be the basis for their decision but decide to subsequently forge ahead with Stage 3 in the method.

There are a few things to consider here. Since Lilly and Larry both think that cost is one of the most important criteria, for this reason, they will use PM5 and defer dealing with cost until Stage 5. In the first four stages, they will consider the functional criteria and the actual characteristics of each option.

Another important point is that it has long been known that people find it difficult to keep more than five to seven things in their minds

Table 6.2 The Argument Matrix

	AREA/LOCATION	PLANNING/INDOOR COMFORT	...

A-STREET NO.1	Rather run-down area
	Far from town but access
	    seems fast
	    ...
		Cosy living room
		Plenty of room for Fido
		...
			...

B-ALLEY NO.2	Far from town and access
	    seems slow
	    ...
		Fantastic terrace
		Own study
		...
			...

...	...	...	...

simultaneously. For this reason, but also because in practice only a few criteria dominate most decision-making situations, they will limit themselves to four criteria (or groups of criteria), with an additional Miscellaneous group for any remaining criteria, as well as an intuition criterion that we will discuss later. Thus, six criteria in all. While this is not the limit of the method, it is a general recommendation not to exceed that.

So, the purpose of Stage 2 is to find four main criteria in the current decision situation. If we regard the previous stage as a brainstorming process, then this stage can be regarded as a process where we ask ourselves what we really want. What do we actually value and appreciate about an option that is a candidate solution to our decision problem? Here, in Stage 2, we construct a matrix in which the options form rows and criteria form columns.

Next, we place each argument from the P-C lists in a box (row and column intersection). If an argument does not fit in any of the regular criteria columns, then place it in the miscellaneous column. A test that the criteria are properly selected is that most of the arguments from the lists fit into one of the four criteria columns and that few or relatively insignificant arguments end up in the miscellaneous column. When the arguments from the P-C lists are categorised, you should carry out the following completion measure. It is possible that one or more boxes in the four criteria columns are empty, in which case they need to be filled in with how we value the respective options under that criterion. (The miscellaneous column need not be filled in the same way.) After this procedure, there is a more complete basis for decisions in which all options are valued under each relevant criterion. You now have a matrix (table) with options you could accept as final choices, and which you have assessed using all the criteria. If you intend to continue with the next stage in the Pilot Method, then you have now completed Stage 2.

6.4 Finishing after Stage 2

But if you already want to try to make your decision at this stage, then one finishing step remains. This step is to pitch the options of the matrix against each other in a way similar to Stage 1 but with more and better-structured information. That they are already in the form of a matrix makes it considerably easier to find an option that is worse than all of the others (if there is such a one) and then eliminate it. If you find several inferior options, then eliminate them all in the same way as we did in Stage 1. Continue this process until you only have two options left. Now do the same as in Stage 1 and take a break. When you return, try to find convincing arguments supporting that this option should be chosen. The option that clearly wins this challenge is the option you should choose from Stage 2. If Lilly and Larry are beguiled by the living room and are happy that Fido has more space, but care neither about the terrace nor the surroundings, they should choose A-street No. 1.

If you also find the last process in this stage relatively tricky, that is because it is too, albeit somewhat less. And that is why there are three more stages in the Pilot Method that help you to find the best option.

6.5 Stage 3 – Ranking the Alternatives

In Stage 1, we produced a set of options and a list of pros and cons (the P-C lists) for each option. In Stage 2, we continued with value assessments. Each option was valued under the four criteria that we considered most important for the decision situation. The P-C lists support this process, which we documented in matrix form (tabular form) where we reviewed each option against each criterion.

Now in Stage 3, we will rank all the options within each criterion separately. Usually, an option we consider the best under one criterion is not the best under all other criteria. If any option were the best under all criteria, the decision would be easy, but this is rarely the case. And in those rare cases, the best option is usually obvious without us needing to conduct any decision analysis at all.

Our example continues (Stage 3): Lilly and Larry were pretty drained after the two initial stages which entailed a considerable effort when they needed to find such a complete set of pros and cons for each of the six apartments. During the coffee break before they started with Stage 3, they speculated over which of the apartments would probably turn out to be best when they were finished with the functional analysis. It is important to remember that this yet only includes functions and properties, not costs, since they use PM5. They concluded that C-road No. 3 and E-avenue No. 5 would probably lead, but it was impossible to say which of them had the advantage. They intuitively ranked the two options equally. They guessed A-street No. 1 as the next one followed by D-crescent No. 4 and F-square No. 6, with B-alley No. 2 last. This order was just their gut feeling ensuing the first two stages, once they had familiarised themselves in depth with their options.

Before we begin to rank the alternatives, we should therefore try to make use of this kind of subconscious information. Sometimes it is not easy to completely describe a decision situation with a set of regular criteria. Even if you are relatively satisfied with the descriptions in the argument matrix in Stage 2, there may be a sense that something is missing. Sometimes there is this sense, but sometimes there is not. This will be different for different people who have different levels of awareness of their thought processes, and it may also be different depending on the decision situation. The Pilot Method is an opportunity to ensure that all such information is exploited. This is an opportunity you can choose to use, but it is not required. Anyone who thinks this sounds vague or does not feel comfortable with it can skip this step. Others should do the following: try to construct an overall ranking of the alternatives based on your gut feeling – what you think or guess the outcome of the functional analysis of the decision will turn out to be. This ranking is called the intuition criterion.

If we assume that options are best under different criteria, then we must rank them for each criterion. By studying our evaluations from Stage 2 in the matrix one column at a time, we can construct a hierarchy. In this hierarchy, we expect to decide which options are better than which others, but a draw is also permitted and indicated by two or more options being ranked with the same placement in the order. After each criterion has been treated separately, you'll have four rankings, one for each of the four criteria, plus the Miscellaneous criterion.

Our example again: Lilly and Larry have come up with a matrix (table) describing how they value their six prospective apartments under the six criteria that are relevant to this decision. Now it is time to look at each criterion separately and rate the options accordingly. They begin with Area/Location; the six alternative apartments are located in different areas and with different locations in these areas. Some are more centrally located, and others are closer to the water. Still others are closer to the socially significant presence of cafes, restaurants, cinemas, and so on. After some discussion, they succeed in ranking the apartments. They rate C-road No. 3 best in terms of Area/Location followed by E-avenue No. 5 and F-square No. 6, followed by the other three apartments ranked in decreasing attractiveness. Then, they do the same with each of the other three criteria: Planning/Indoor comfort, School, and Commuting/Accessibility. The same apartment will not lead in all criteria. For example, C-road No. 3 is the penultimate for Floor plan but is first for Area/Location. Finally, they rank the remaining factors which did not fall under the four main criteria. At this stage, Lilly and Larry feel that their criteria have become stable clusters of aspects and they rename them accordingly as Neighbourhood, Floor plan, School, and Travel, respectively.

Now it is time to score the rankings of the alternatives. This is entirely mechanical and involves no opinion or consideration. All that is needed is pen and paper or an Excel spreadsheet that is produced in a matter of minutes. In the matrix that contains the option rows and criteria columns, points are awarded systematically so that under each criterion the worst option gets 1 point, the second worst 2 points, and so on up to the best option.

Back to our example: Draws between options are allowed, but for Lilly and Larry, there are no draws in which two options are ranked the same except under the intuitive criterion. You can see their rankings in Table 6.3. As a very preliminary result, the options' scores are summed across the rows which put C-road in first place followed by E-avenue and A-street. This summary does not consider how the criteria are of different importance but rather considers all aspects as equally important. This is not something that Lilly and Larry actually agree on. And the fact that no option is best under all criteria, but rather that options so to speak cross over under the different criteria,

Table 6.3 Stage 3 in the Pilot Method – Ranking Alternatives

STAGE 3	NEIGHBOURHOOD	FLOOR PLAN	SCHOOL	TRAVEL	MISC.	INTUITION	RESULT
A-STREET NO.1	1	4	6	3	4	3	21
B-ALLEY NO.2	3	6	1	1	2	1	14
C-ROAD NO.3	6	2	4	4	6	4	26
D-CRESCENT NO.4	2	5	3	2	3	2	17
E-AVENUE NO.5	5	3	5	6	1	4	24
F-SQUARE NO.6	4	1	2	5	5	2	19

means that Lilly and Larry decide to proceed to the next stage in the method. Thus, Table 6.3 shows the intermediate result of this stage. Note that rows and columns switch places compared to Stage 2 since this stage is a numerical one.

More generally, in Stage 3, the lowest ranked item under each criterion receives 1 point, the second lowest ranking receives 2 points, and so on, up to the highest ranking which receives as many points as there are alternatives. An exception is if two or more options are ranked equally under any criterion, then they get the same score but a higher ranking will still only get one point more than the option ranked immediately below. You will now have a column with points for all options under each criterion. However, note here that we have not taken into account how important the criteria are. If you intend to do this by continuing with Stage 4 in the Pilot Method, you are now finished with Stage 3.

6.6 Finishing after Stage 3

But if you already want to try to make a decision in Stage 3, then one finishing step remains. This step is to sum the options by row. We summarise the scores each option received across all criteria and obtain a total. The option with the highest total is the option that the Pilot Method Pilot indicates is the best, but since we are only at Stage 3, it is good to take the results with a pinch of salt. At least retain the two or three best options and try to reason which option is preferable using a procedure similar to the previous two stages. Remember, so far, we have ranked only the alternatives, not the criteria. Ranking the criteria, which comes next, is an important component of the Pilot Method. But at the 2013 EURO-INFORMS joint research conference in Rome, Don Kleinmuntz of Strata Decisions presented an MCDA decision-making software tool that was bought and used by over 1,000 hospitals in the United States. It contained a number of criteria that were by default set at equal weights (i.e. in essence no conscious weighting) and supposed to be altered by each hospital individually according to their particular preferences and priorities. In reality, it turned out that less than 10 of those over 1,000 hospitals actually changed the weights at all (in our terminology, went beyond Stage 3) and declared themselves satisfied with the decision support they had received that far. This is not to say that you should not move on to the next stage if your decision is not yet finalised, you definitely should, but rather that there are considerable knowledge gains at every stage of the Pilot Method.

6.7 Stage 4 – Ranking the Criteria

In Stage 1, we produced a set of options, and we developed a list of pros and cons for each option. In Stage 2, we continued by assessing the options. Each option was evaluated under the four criteria we selected for the current decision situation. All these were documented in the form of a matrix in which we ensured that each option was judged under each criterion. In Stage 3, we then ranked the alternatives within each criterion so that we had as many rankings as we had criteria.

The result from Stage 3 was a scored matrix where each option under each criterion has a score that indicates exactly how this option has been ranked under the current criterion. A higher score indicates that the item is placed higher in the ranking, while a score of 1 point indicates that the option ranked last of all the options under this particular criterion. But the summation made in Stage 3 did not take into account that some criteria are more important than others. Therefore, time is nigh for ranking the criteria, not unlike the procedure we did for the options in Stage 3.

Our example again (Stage 4): Lilly and Larry have now done most of the work with evaluating their options under the criteria they selected. As we have seen, both of them felt that they had listed the criteria roughly in their order of importance: Neighbourhood, Floor plan, School, Travel, and Miscellaneous. However, when using the Pilot Method, they need to decide exactly what their thoughts are about the criteria *in the current decision situation*. They need to decide how important the different criteria are *in this particular case*.

When Larry and Lilly look at the six options, they feel that their locations are actually all quite ok. Although there are differences, they are not extremely large. The same goes for the floor plans and indoor comfort. They realise that within their price range, they will have neither a big living room nor a recently modernised kitchen, so the differences are not so great between the options they have selected and are currently considering. However, the schools in different areas clearly differ substantially, and both Lilly and Larry are keen that Fido will get a good education throughout elementary school. Larry works as an IT consultant which means that he is periodically leased out to customers that can be virtually anywhere in the city. If the apartment they choose is too far from the beaten track, Larry risks having to make some very long commuting trips, and when they look again they realise that this is an essential difference between the various options.

After rethinking this, Lilly and Larry realise that the difference between the best and worst options for the School criterion is the most important in this particular decision situation followed by Travel, Neighbourhood, and Floor plan in that order. Again, this order does not mean that Floor plan is less important than School in any absolute sense, only that Lilly and Larry have taken a stand specific to the current situation. Thus, their real criteria ranking differs markedly from what they initially thought it would be. They had not realised that such a ranking must be relative to the options – it cannot be absolute in any sense.

It is important to note two crucial differences compared to Stage 3. First, criteria are ranked only once, not numerous rankings as was the case with the options. Second, this ranking is relative, which is a very important point. The statement "criterion A is more important than criterion B" is irrelevant in this form because we do not know what options are available under these criteria. Let us reconnect back to the flashlight example in the previous chapter and discuss a similar situation. Suppose someone says that for computer hard disk drives "price is more important than storage capacity." But if the prices of three disks under consideration are $50, $55, and $60 with storage capacities 1,000 GB, 2,000 GB, and 3,000 GB, the decision is completely different than if prices were $50, $70, and $90 for hard drives with storage capacities 1,300 GB, 1,400 GB, and 1,500 GB. Basically, no matter how we weigh price in relation to capacity, we choose the last hard drive in the first of these two examples and the first one in the second. To sum up: *the key is to rank the criteria according to the differences between the options in all criteria.*

In the first example, only $10 distinguishes 2,000 GB of storage capacity and in the second $40 distinguishes 200 GB. It is these differences we must pitch against each other, not the absolute values themselves. "Price is more important than storage capacity" is therefore insufficient information to proceed with in a decision analysis. Such a statement will lead you completely astray. When we have to rank the criteria, it is hence important to rank the respective ranges between the best and worst options under each criterion. It is exactly here that many decision-makers fail, so this stage deserves to be taken very seriously. This also entails that should you go back to Stage 3 at any point and change the rankings of options under one or more criteria, the criteria ranking in this stage must subsequently be revisited.

Our main example again: Lilly and Larry have agreed on the ranking of criteria: School, Travel, Neighbourhood, and Floor plan in that order based on the actual differences between their available options, not based on any absolute truth or order regardless of the options, simply because no such truth can exist. Therefore, they assign weights as follows: Floor plan 1 point, Neighbourhood 2 points, Travel 3 points, and finally 4 points to School. Then, they multiply the options' points with their respective weights and sum for each option, see Table 6.4. In this way, they gain an overall score for each option and that score is their complete evaluation of each option. The highest score thus indicates the option that Lilly and Larry should prefer if they had a free choice, i.e. if there were no costs involved. In Table 6.4, we can see that E-avenue No. 5 and C-street No. 3 have changed places compared with Stage 3.

In general, after ranking the criteria, it is time to score them (in the previous stage, we assigned points to options, not criteria). The least important of the criteria receives weight 1; the next, weight 2; and up to the most important, which receives the highest weight. If two criteria are deemed equally important, assign the same weight as we did with points for the options in the previous stage. Once the criteria are assigned weights, sum up each option's total score as we

Table 6.4 Ranking Criteria without the Intuition Criterion

RELATIVE WEIGHTS STAGE 4	2 NEIGHBOURHOOD	1 FLOOR PLAN	4 SCHOOL	3 TRAVEL	1 MISC.	0 INTUITION	RESULT
A-ROAD NO.1	2	4	24	9	4	0	43
B-ALLEY NO.2	6	6	4	3	2	0	21
C-STREET NO.3	12	2	16	12	6	0	48
D-CRESCENT NO.4	4	5	12	6	3	0	30
E-AVENUE NO.5	10	3	20	18	1	0	52
F-SQUARE NO.6	8	1	8	15	5	0	37

did in Stage 3. But before summing, each option's score in the table is multiplied by the weight that each criterion received. If you have a Miscellaneous criterion in which you have a number of smaller aspects that you still want to include in the analysis, assign the weight 1 to Miscellaneous, otherwise assign 0.

For example, the score for A-road No. 1 is calculated as $2 \cdot 1 + 1 \cdot 4 + 4 \cdot 6 + 3 \cdot 3 + 1 \cdot 4 + 0 \cdot 3 = 2 + 4 + 24 + 9 + 4 + 0 = 43$.

In doing this, something remarkable happens. From our many years of research and development of decision methods, including algorithm development and mathematical simulations of all kinds of decision situations, as well as numerous real-life decisions analyses, we find that this relatively simple rating method we have just explained imposes a strongly discriminatory (decisive) effect on the decision analysis. One would think that specifying exact percentages for weights would be important or identifying them more precisely should be. But a straight ranking order has proved to have properties that are close to as good – with a lot less effort. As we discussed earlier, it is generally very difficult or even impossible to give such weights with any real precision anyhow, and in such cases, ranking proves to be the superior method for indicating the importance of various criteria.

The total score for each option in this process is the final ranking of the functional quality and capacity of the options being considered in the decision situation if you follow PM5 and of the entire option for PM4. Stage 4 is hereby completed, and if we follow PM4 or if there is no cost component in the analysis, then we have reached a final decision. Otherwise, we need to proceed to Stage 5.

6.8 Finishing after Stage 4

But before we do, those who took the opportunity to set up an intuition criterion may use it now, simply by comparing its ranking with that resulting from Stage 4 in which the intuition criterion was assigned the weight 0, as in the example with Larry and Lilly in Table 6.4. If the rankings are consistent or almost consistent with each other, there seems to be no significant difference between the gut feeling and the formal results of the analysis. If the rankings are not consistent, there is subliminal information that partly contradicts the results of the analysis. Such a discrepancy does not mean that the analysis is

Table 6.5 Ranking Criteria with the Intuition Criterion Activated

RELATIVE WEIGHTS STAGE 4	2 NEIGHBOURHOOD	1 FLOOR PLAN	4 SCHOOL	3 TRAVEL	1 MISC.	1 INTUITION	RESULT
A-ROAD NO.1	2	4	24	9	4	3	46
B-ALLEY NO.2	6	6	4	3	2	1	22
C-STREET NO.3	12	2	16	12	6	4	52
D-CRESCENT NO.4	4	5	12	6	3	2	32
E-AVENUE NO.5	10	3	20	18	1	4	56
F-SQUARE NO.6	8	1	8	15	5	2	39

wrong. Either the conception represented by gut feeling is misplaced, which is common, or it indicates that some criterion has been overlooked or that an option has been badly ranked. The analysis should then go back to Stage 1 or 2 to see if there is any reason to re-evaluate the work of those stages. But before going back, it is advisable to check on the size of the deviation. This is done by increasing the weight of the intuition criterion in increments of one until reaching five. At weight 5, gut feeling weighs more than the main criterion and if the analysis still has not flipped to the expected result, then we can say with great certainty that our gut feeling is playing tricks on us.

Back to our example: Lilly's and Larry's intuitive ranking corresponded fairly well with the formal analysis, but there were some small differences with options that they could not distinguish and yet which clearly differed in the analysis. Because they believe that buying an apartment is a decision that should be both close to optimal and also feel right, they choose in Table 6.5 to include their intuition criterion and assign it a weight of 1, thus including it in the result of the stage.

6.9 Stage 5 – Separate Cost Analysis

In its large PM5 form, the Pilot Method consists of five stages, so this is the last one. In Stages 1 and 2, we produced a set of options and evaluated each of them. Each option was evaluated under the four criteria that were selected for the decision situation. Then in Stage 3, options were ranked under each criterion, and in Stage 4, criteria were weighted in relation to each other. The total score each option received in Stage 4 was the final ranking of the functional quality of the options. This leaves only the matter of cost to analyse in Stage 5.

Table 6.6   Trading Cost and Functionality

STAGE 5	COST/MONTH	COST INCREASE	SCORE DIFFERENCE	DOMINANCE
A-ROAD NO.1	1590	310	+24	Dominated
B-ALLEY NO.2	1280	0	0	← Base case
C-STREET NO.3	1550	270	+30	
D-CRESCENT NO.4	1490	210	+10	Dominated
E-AVENUE NO.5	1710	430	+34	
F-SQUARE NO.6	1430	150	+17	

Back to our example (Stage 5): Lilly and Larry have conducted an analysis of six apartments according to the previous stage. For each option, they have calculated a monthly expense based on the monthly fee plus interest on the loans they would need to take. They calculate using a fixed rate for the next few years in order to obtain a secure budget. The cost per month for the six options is shown in Table 6.6.

Lilly and Larry want to keep costs down, so they start with the least expensive option. They take that option as the basis of their analysis and thus make B-alley No. 2 their so-called base case. In two columns in Table 6.6, they then work out how much more than the base case each option will cost and how many more points these have. It is possible that an option can have fewer points than the base case, which would yield a negative point difference, but this is not so in their case. Before they begin with the monetary analysis, they look to see whether any options are dominated, i.e. any options that score lower in points for a higher cost than some other option. They see fairly quickly that A-road No. 1 is both more expensive than and inferior to C-street No. 3 and likewise that D-crescent No. 4 is both more expensive than and inferior to F-square No. 6. Two options can therefore be rejected before the analysis in this stage has even begun.

Starting with the base case B-alley No. 2, Lilly and Larry now analyse what they can get for their money if they decide to invest more. They look at the options in ascending order of cost. For $150/ month more than the base scenario, they can live on F-square No. 6, an increase of 17 functional points. When they pitch these two options against each other, F-square seems much more interesting and worth the difference in cost, so they decide to keep it and reject the base case B-alley No. 2. Next, they compare F-square No. 6 to the cheapest remaining option that hasn't yet been rejected, which is C-street No. 3. For a further increase of $120/month, a total of $270 above the (rejected) base case, they get an apartment they found to have 30 more points, a further increase of 13 functional points. Here, Lilly is a little hesitant but Larry is more positive. After a discussion, they find that even this improvement is worth taking, so C-street becomes their new choice. There is now only one option left to consider, E-avenue No. 5. At $160/month more than C-street, and a total of $430/month above the base case, they can acquire an apartment they valued 34 points better than the base case, a meagre 4 points more than C-street. That difference between the two options does not seem that great to them, and altogether, C-street appears to be the most value for money.

The decision really could only have turned out two ways during this analysis. Both of them were convinced that F-square was considerably more value for money than B-alley, but maybe Lilly could have convinced Larry that they should not have chosen C-street. Both were in complete agreement that they gained a superior overview of the decision situation by using the Pilot Method and that with good factual arguments, it was relatively easy to arrive at the evaluation shown in Table 6.6 and then at a decision that they were both happy with and feel they understood.

To be a little more general, a mechanism in classical cost-benefit analysis is that costs and benefits are pitched against each other while seeking the greatest possible differences on the benefit side. And the idea behind Analysis of Benefits and Costs (ABC) in decision contexts is the same. You look for the option that provides the greatest difference between functionality and costs, i.e. what colloquially would be called the most value for money. We highlighted the functionality/benefits in the four previous stages of the method, and they are indicated by the sum of the points from Stage 4. In order to compare the functionality benefits to the costs, we need to find a way to compare points to monetary terms. After having rejected options that are dominated, i.e. they have a higher cost and worse functionality score than one other option, the following procedure should be followed:

- We cannot reduce the cost below the least expensive option. Therefore, we use that as the base case for the procedure. Let the cost of the least expensive option be M dollars.

- For each option, the increased cost is now calculated. If the cost of an alternative is P dollars, then the increased cost will be P − M dollars. This difference should be set against the corresponding difference for each option in the final functionality score in Stage 4 compared with the score of the base scenario.
- For each such pair-wise comparison, the most cost-effective and affordable option is retained and the other rejected.
- This procedure is repeated for each option that is still not rejected from the lowest to the highest cost.
- When all the options but one has been rejected, only the most cost-effective and affordable option remains and that is the one to choose.

These bullet points describe an approximate procedure because it contains subjective estimates of characteristics that are not easily quantifiable, but this is the method's strength rather than its weakness. It is impossible to accurately determine an objective estimate of functional points. Even if it were possible, such a procedure would take an unreasonably long time to carry out and require considerable resources. Instead, the points should be seen as stable and good indicators for the stated preferences and values so that when Stage 5 finally pitches costs against features and functions, it does so using real costs against real functionality for the options.

Our example for the last time: After having used the Pilot Method, Lilly and Larry decide to select the apartment on C-street. The following week, they sign the contract for the apartment on the top floor of C-street No. 3. Then, they live happily ever after and their son Fido has a wonderful childhood and in due course a great career as a management consultant. Furthermore, their dog Smilla avoids the crowded parks in the town centre and has access to large recreation areas.

The Pilot Method is an iterative method even if only one cycle has been described in this chapter. When new information arrives or the set of options change, the stages should be revisited accordingly. Feel free to iterate back to any stage at any time, but remember that once a stage is revisited, all ensuing stages must be revisited in sequence before the new iteration is completed. This is especially important for the criteria ranking in Stage 4.

6.10 Summary

The Pilot Method is one of the easiest decision methods that is still powerful enough, not least procedurally speaking but also in terms of obtaining stable and transparent results. It is the culmination of many years of research and development that has shifted from very powerful and also very complex methods to progressively simpler ones, both in terms of user interfaces and calculations, but without losing too much decision power. The Pilot Method has the obvious advantage of being computable by hand or very easily modelled in a computer spreadsheet. More complex methods require either advanced computational software or complex spreadsheet modelling. Thus, one can say that the Pilot Method is the most reasonable combination of simplicity and decision-analytic power available.

Note that decision analyses such as the Pilot Method can be used in two diametrically opposed ways.

- You can perform a forward analysis based on information about a number of options and their properties and try to arrive at a total ranking where one or possibly several options appear to be the most advantageous.
- Or an inverse analysis can be carried out, where the goal is to make sure that an agreed-upon decision is good enough. The inverse analysis can involve adjusting weights or other judgement values in order for the results to match and make sense.

At first glance, an inverse analysis appears a bit fraudulent since there is a danger that the parameters are adjusted to values that they would not have had in a forward analysis based on known facts. But since the purpose of an inverted analysis is quite different, we should see the work in a different light. The idea here is to try to understand what led to a decision, regardless of whether that means certain parameters take on values that do not appear to be consistent with the worldview that prevails at the time of the analysis in the mind of the decision-maker. Through an inverse analysis, we can find out how and what is valued, in a way that in retrospect does not seem to be optimal, or if there simply are real disagreements about certain data inputs. This can be of great value, but it should not be confused with the process in a forward ("normal") analysis. Both analytical methods are supported by the Pilot Method, and they both work in a completely analogous way. We have, however, in this chapter, focused on the more commonly used forward analysis.

7

REAL-LIFE CASE STUDIES

In this chapter, we briefly exemplify some of the methods described in this book with three different large domain applications in which we have been involved and where we have carried out extensive decision analyses.

1. An example of how to improve procurement processes and how to use qualitative data regarding contractors under different criteria to select one.
2. A complex policy formation regarding hazardous societal events, exemplified by an evaluation of different mitigation measures when several stakeholders and criteria are involved in the formation process as well as how to form adequate societal response strategies to catastrophic events, even under significant uncertainties.
3. An analysis of energy transition and electricity generation policies in Jordan for the next 30 years from the perspective that it must provide a sustainable solution that is acceptable to a wide range of stakeholders with potentially conflicting opinions.

While these cases are all high-profile societal cases, this does not indicate that the methods in this book are more suited to such cases than to smaller or personal life cases. On the contrary, the methods work as well with any size of decision situation, and in Chapter 8, we will summarise and show how to handle decision situations of all sizes.

7.1 Procurement

The monetary values involved in procurements are very high. For instance, public procurements in the OECD countries have an annual turnover of 16–18% of GDP and the amount of money involved is thus staggeringly significant. Unfortunately, without paying adequate attention to the challenges of, say, balancing monetary values against other qualities, the processes often result in questionable assessments

DOI: 10.1201/9781003406709-7
85

and outcomes. One of the main issues is how to handle the relation between qualitative values. Here, we exemplify how pure rankings in a multi-criteria model can be utilised for procurement processes. We use as an example a real-life decision situation in which we were involved that aimed at selecting a contractor for the construction of an academic institution building.

After a tender process, three bids from building contractors *a1*, *a2*, and *a3* were received, all of which were matched against the main criteria stated in the procurement process description:

- *Functionality*: Symbolic value, facilitation of social contacts, access to public facilities, the efficiency of office space, fulfilment of environmental requirements, and technical standards.
- *Location*: Interaction with the local environment and access to common facilities.
- *Change opportunities*: Interaction during the contract phase as well as flexibility during the planning and the contract phases.
- *Contractor responsiveness*: Responsiveness to the needs and innovation capacity of the institution.
- *Price*: The full monetary cost of the building (construction, maintenance, electricity, heating, etc.) over a 10-year period.

The five criteria were further subdivided into a total of 15 sub-criteria. The final rankings after the evaluation process are shown in Table 7.1. The column *Contractor ranking* shows the rankings of the various contractors under the respective sub-criteria. For instance, in sub-criterion 2 (contribution to social contacts), {a1, a2} > a3 means that a1 and a2 were equally good but also that both a1 and a2 were preferred to a3. In the same manner, in sub-criterion 4 (realisation of office space), {a1, a2, a3} means that all contractors were ranked equally good. The column *Sub-Criteria Ranking* shows how the numbered sub-criteria were ranked. For the importance of the sub-criteria under the main criterion Change opportunities, {9, 10} > {11, 12} means that 9 and 10 were considered to be more important than 11 and 12, which, like 9 and 10, were equally important among themselves.

Note that all contractors were ranked under each sub-criterion and then the sub-criteria were ranked according to importance with respect to the differences among the contractors under those sub-criteria. Lastly, the main criteria were ranked with respect to the

Table 7.1 Preference Rankings

CRITERIA AND SUB-CRITERIA	CONTRACTOR RANKING	SUB-CRITERIA RANKING
Functionality		4 > 1 > {2, 3, 5, 6}
1. SYMBOLIC VALUE	a2 > a1 > a3	
2. CONTRIBUTION TO SOCIAL CONTACTS	{a1, a2} > a3	
3. ACCESS TO PUBLIC FACILITIES	a2 > {a1, a3}	
4. REALISATION OF OFFICE SPACE	{a1, a2, a3}	
5. TECHNICAL STANDARD	{a1, a2, a3}	
6. ENVIRONMENTAL REQUIREMENTS	a1 > {a2, a3}	
Location		7 > 8
7. INTERACTION WITH THE ENVIRONMENT	a2 > a3 > a1	
8. ACCESS TO COMMON FACILITIES	a3 > {a1, a2}	
Change opportunities		{9, 10} > {11, 12}
9. INTERACTION DURING THE PLANNING PHASE	a3 > a1 > a2	
10. INTERACTION DURING THE CONTRACT PHASE	{a2, a3} > a1	
11. FLEXIBILITY DURING THE PLANNING PHASE	a3 > a1 > a2	
12. FLEXIBILITY DURING THE CONTRACT PHASE	{a1, a2, a3}	
Contractor responsiveness		14 > 13
13. RESPONSIVENESS	{a1, a2, a3}	
14. INNOVATION	a2 > {a1, a3}	
Cost		
15. COST	{a1, a2, a3}	

relative importance of their sub-criteria, resulting in a ranking of Cost > Functionality > Location > Contractor responsiveness > Change opportunities, where ">" again denotes "is more important than." Figure 7.1 shows the representation of the multi-criteria hierarchy. The evaluation could have been made using the pure Pilot Method, but due to the number of criteria, especially at two different levels, a computer program was used as support. Note that the alternatives are only ranked at the sub-criteria level, and the upper criteria level is only for concatenating and summing up the underlying level.

Figure 7.2 shows the result of the evaluation. In the figure, the higher the bar for an alternative (called strategy in the software), the better it is, given the available information. The interpretation is that a bar with a height of 1 (100% would represent a contractor that is optimal in all criteria and sub-criteria). This is almost invariably not the case, and if

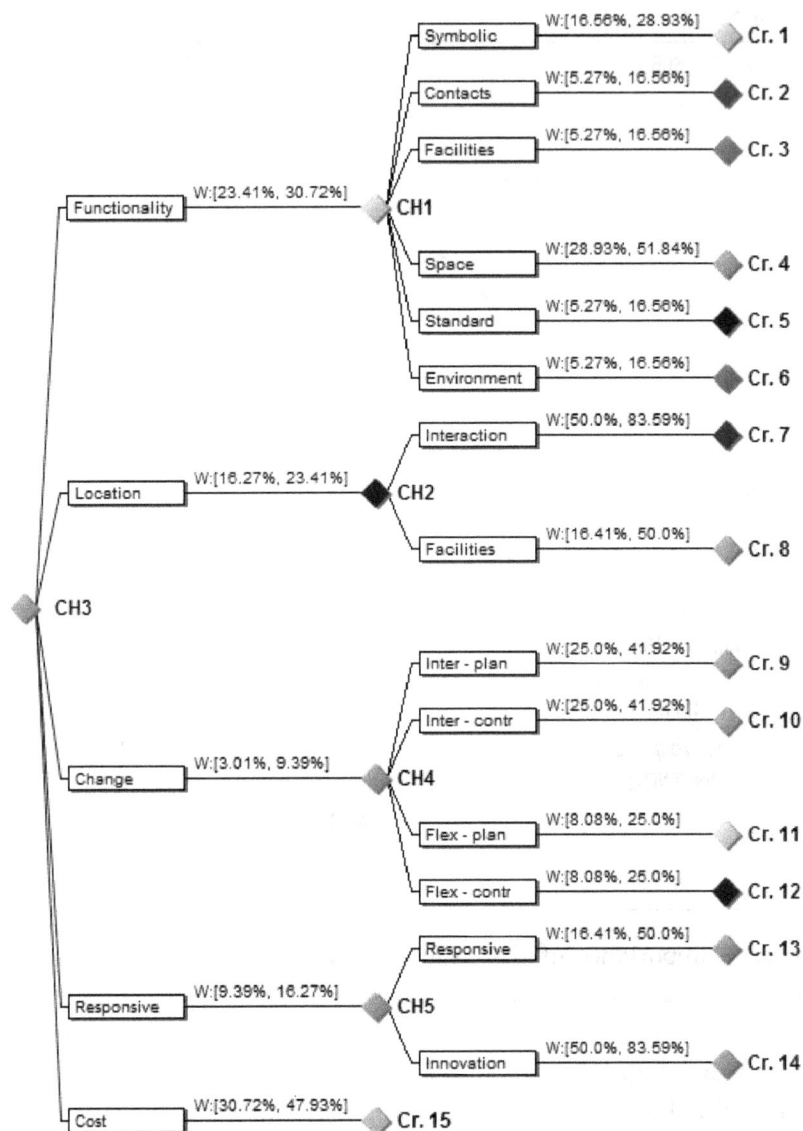

Figure 7.1   The multi-criteria hierarchy of the procurement case where surrogate numbers for the rankings have been calculated.

something even close would be at hand, this would be apparent without an analysis. The different parts that make up the bars also show how much each criterion contributes to the respective results, based on the possible ranges of the resulting weighted averages of the respective contractors. Furthermore, the significance and robustness of the evaluation

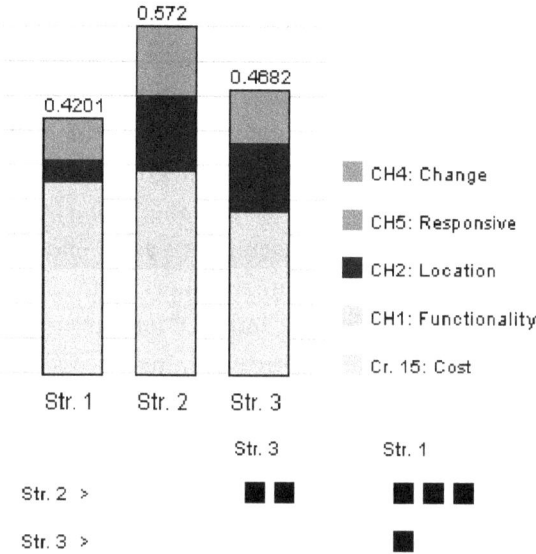

Figure 7.2 The evaluation result of the procurement case.

result are marked by black squares. Three squares mean that there is a significant difference between the features and that there must be substantial changes in the input data for it to change. Two squares mean that there is still a clear difference, but it is more sensitive to variations in the input data. One square means that rather small changes in the data can reverse the ranking between those contractors.

We can see in Figure 7.2 that contractor a2 (Strategy 2) is clearly the best with a margin of more than 10% of an ideal imagined contractor followed by a3 and a1. The confidence with which this can be stated is shown in the lower part of the figure. That a2 is to prefer to a3 can be said with confidence (75–90% of the belief in that statement falls on a2) and that a2 is to prefer to a1 can be said with high confidence (over 90% of the belief in that statement falls on a2).

7.2 Policy Formation for Catastrophic Events

The rather recent outbreak of the Covid-19 pandemic highlighted the fact that many countries did not anticipate such a situation and were thusly not well-prepared. Decision-makers had to operate in conditions of severe uncertainty about, e.g., fatality rates, spread, timing of infectiousness, and number of asymptomatic cases.

Thus, few decision-makers did have reliable information about the best measures to protect society. As became evident in many countries, there seemed to be no prepared strategies in advance for such a dramatic scenario since many countries acted in seemingly rather uncoordinated manners, at least at the beginning of the pandemic. Many countermeasures did severely limit individual freedom and carried significant economic and societal costs as an effect of the single-criterion aim to avoid fatalities in the short term, even though the measures were at risk of having indirect long-term effects such as economic recession in various degrees, limited access to education, as well as other effects on a large number of socioeconomic factors.

Rather than looking only at epidemiologic and healthcare factors, our purpose, in this case, was to model and evaluate policy problems by also including socioeconomic factors in a multi-criteria and multi-stakeholder context. The decision model was applied in Botswana, Jordan, and Romania and can also be used in handling future crisis situations at a societal level, to facilitate the management and mitigation of similar crisis situations in the future in any region, while providing recommendations for the assessment and evaluation of different scenarios and their impacts for analysing various policies, alternatives, and trade-offs under conditions of strong uncertainty.

A fundamental component in this model is a set of criteria under which the various options are considered. The options are valued under each criterion, and the relative importance of the criteria themselves are thereafter determined. For demonstration purposes, consider the following criteria (see Figure 7.3 and Table 7.2):

- Number of cases (critical, severe, and mild)
- Economic aspects (two sub-criteria)
- Social and behavioural (four sub-criteria)
- Political and governance (two sub-criteria)

Typical mitigation measures are partitioned into sets with different subordinate restriction levels, reflecting some important aspects of possible mitigation strategies on different levels:

- *Level L1*: A scenario in which no other action is taken except pharmaceutical measures and case isolation.
- *Level L2*: A basic influenza epidemic protocol.

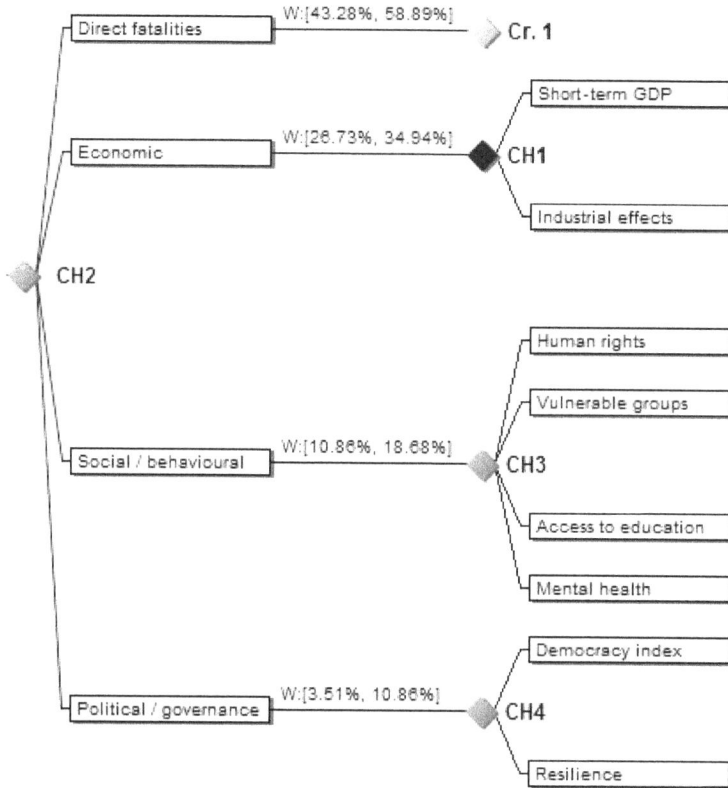

Figure 7.3 The multi-criteria hierarchy for policy formation.

- *Level L3*: Mild social distancing measures (large public gatherings banned, work from home where possible, and social distancing).
- *Level L4*: Partial lockdown – imposed social distancing measures and restrictions on mobility.

Other values are tentatively estimated but should in an extended analysis be refined based on economic models, empirical data, more well-deliberated qualified estimates, etc., when those become available.

The (limited a priori) criteria ranking from the questionnaire results could be summarised as health considerations being more important than the economy, which is more important than human rights, which in turn is more important than educational aspects. This is an ordinal ranking of the criteria taking the respective ranges between best and worst under each criterion into account:

Table 7.2 The Value Estimates for the Respective Measure under Each Criterion, Collected from the Case of Romania.

CRITERION / MEASURE	HEALTH	ECONOMIC		SOCIAL AND BEHAVIOURAL				POLITICAL AND GOVERNANCE	
	DIRECT FATALITIES	SHORT-TERM COSTS	IMPACT ON SPECIFIC INDUSTRIES	HUMAN RIGHTS	VULNERABLE GROUPS	ACCESS TO EDUCATION	MENTAL HEALTH	RISK OF ABUSES	RESILIENCE
LEVEL L1	29400–36000	1–3	Better than L2	Better than L2	1.4	0	Better than L2	6.49	47.9
LEVEL L2	30700–37600	1–4	Better than L3	Better than L3	1.4	14–28	Better than L3	6.49	44.9
LEVEL L3	19800–24100	3–5	Much better than L4	Better than L4	1.6	0	Better than L4	6.44	50.9
LEVEL L4	25800–31600	5–6			1.7	54–84		6.4	41.9

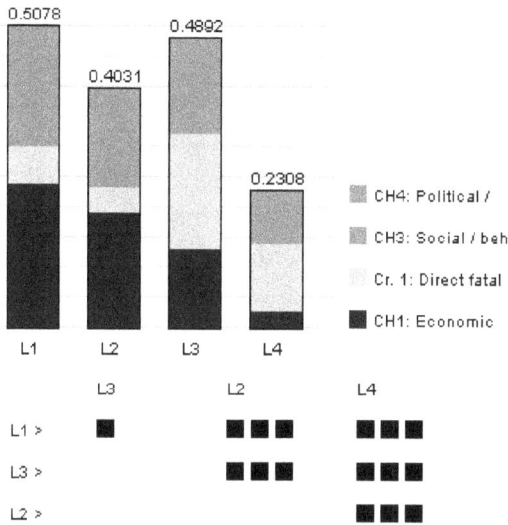

Figure 7.4 The result of a multi-criteria evaluation of the Romanian case.

- The maximum difference between L1 and L4 in Cases is more important than the maximum difference between L1 and L4 in Economy.
- The maximum difference between L1 and L4 in Economy is more important than the maximum difference between L1 and L4 in Human rights.
- The maximum difference between L1 and L4 in Human rights is more important than the maximum difference between L1 and L4 in Education.

From Figure 7.4, we can see that the difference between L3 (highest score) and L1 is rather small (and has only one black square, i.e. does not reach 75% confidence), but these two alternatives seem to be the best courses of action. Furthermore, this result is comparatively robust since with more than 90% confidence (three squares), those two are significantly better than L2 which follows closest.

7.3 Energy Planning

Energy supply policy planning is of prime concern to any modern nation. The Jordanian government was in 2018 considering a number of electricity-generating technologies to be used alongside imported energy. The energy policy in Jordan aims to address both climate change mitigation and energy security by increasing the share of low-carbon technologies and domestically available resources. Existing technologies include the scaling up of renewable energy sources, the use of nuclear energy, and shale oil exploration. However, the views, perceptions, and opinions regarding these technologies – their benefits, risks, and costs – varied significantly among different stakeholder groups inside and outside of Jordan.

We present the results of a four-year project that included extensive stakeholder processes. The data were collected during stakeholder processes in three major steps: (i) expert views by providing large-scale online surveys for energy experts in Jordan, (ii) stakeholder views collected in six workshops with homogenous groups of stakeholders, and (iii) stakeholder views at a final workshop with mixed groups of stakeholders.

There were seven different groups of stakeholders, see Table 7.3. In total, there were 72 stakeholders among the different groups participating in the workshop steps (ii) and (iii). Altogether, there were 11 criteria in the analyses, see Table 7.4 and Figure 7.5.

The following nine feasible national technology strategies were evaluated under the criteria, see Table 7.5. Figure 7.6 shows the final criteria ranking and the energy technologies under the respective criteria. The figure presents the final result of the evaluation of the decision problem. We can see that alternative 1 (local solar power) definitely is the most preferable option with more than 90% confidence (three squares). It is followed by alternative 2 (central solar power, CSP) and alternative 3 (nuclear power) which are practically indistinguishable in the total analysis even though they have their strengths in different

Table 7.3 Stakeholder Groups

- Policymakers: the Jordanian government and organisations responsible for developing and implementing energy policies in Jordan.
- Finance and industry: energy and engineering companies as well as banks.
- Academia: researchers and academics in the energy domain.
- Young leaders: students in the field of energy and young employees at energy companies, power plants, etc.
- NGOs in the energy, environment, and engineering fields.
- Civil society and national non-governmental organisations.
- Local communities: representatives from different cities where infrastructure projects are planned.

Table 7.4   Criteria

1. Use of domestic energy sources. (If possible, use local natural resources rather than imported ones).
2. Global warming potential.
3. Domestic value chain. (The technology should have a high potential to use components and services provided by domestic industries.)
4. Technology and knowledge transfer. (Potential to benefit future domestic development.)
5. Electricity system costs. (Total costs from construction and maintenance.)
6. On-site job creation. (Jobs directly or indirectly created from each energy source.)
7. Pressure on local land resources. (Minimise the additional pressure on valuable land resources.)
8. Pressure on local water security. (Water is very scarce in Jordan and continuous supply is critical.)
9. Occurrence and manageability of non-emission hazardous waste. (Minimise the disposal of non-emission hazardous waste.)
10. Local air pollution and health. (Minimise the amount of air pollutants.)
11. Safety. (Minimise the risk of severe accidents in the production chain.)

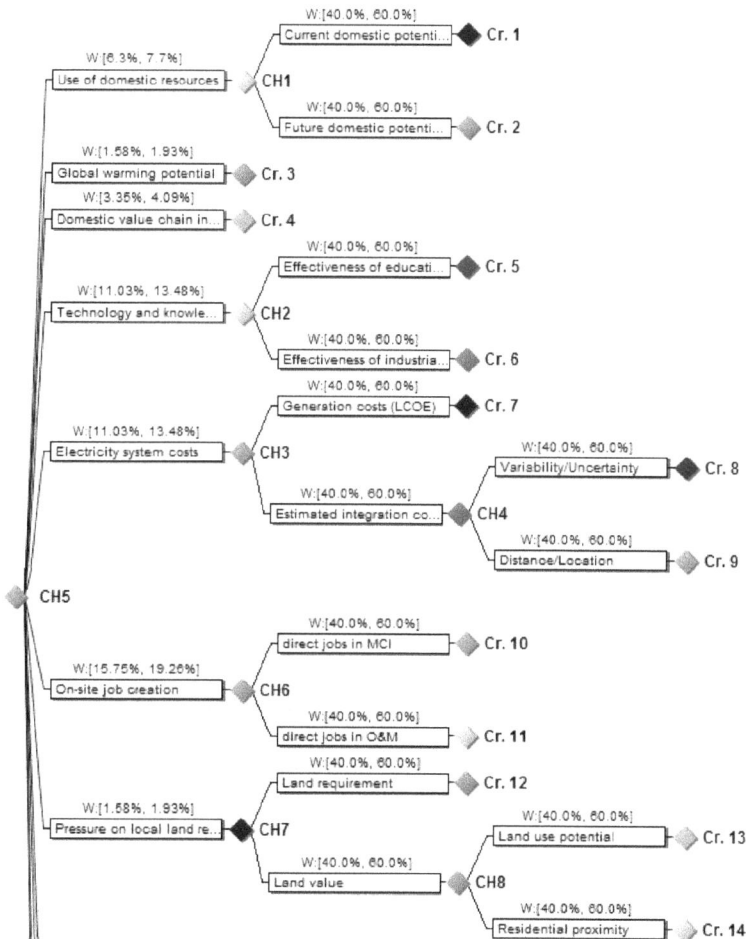

Figure 7.5 The multi-criteria hierarchy for energy planning. *(Continued)*

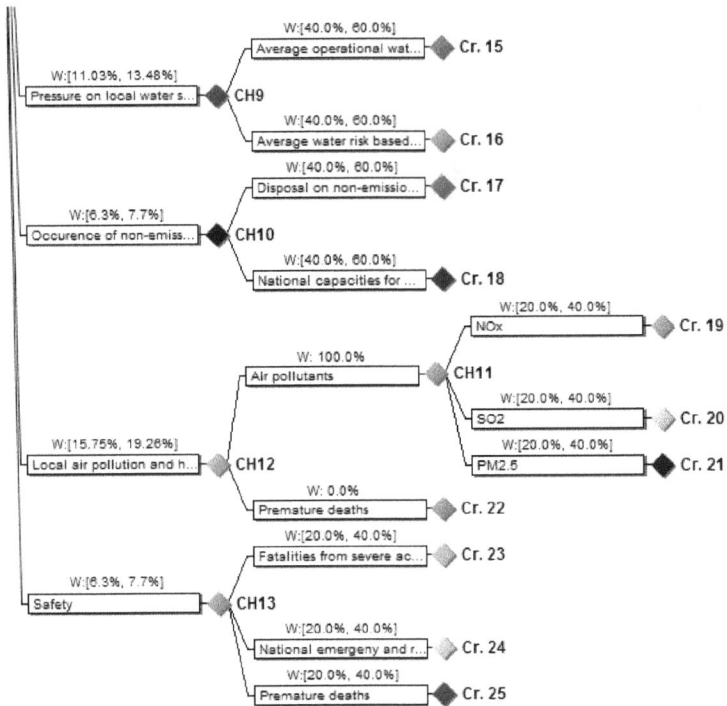

Figure 7.5 *(Continued)*

criteria. Alternative 1 (local solar power) is at least as good as most of the other technologies on most criteria and often clearly better. For example, the criterion Local air pollution is playing an important role in all technologies and the criterion Job creation is important for, among others, oil shale.

The insights and results that came out of the decision analysis were not realised before the final workshop where the negotiations took place and the final analysis was made. It was only after two rounds of stakeholder negotiations, using this methodology, that the results

Table 7.5   Nine Technology Strategies

- Solar power: 1. Local (utility PV) and 2. Concentrated/centralised (CSP)
- 3. Onshore wind power
- 4. Hydroelectric power
- 5. Nuclear power
- Fossil fuels: 6. Coal, 7. Gas, 8. Oil, and 9. Oil shale

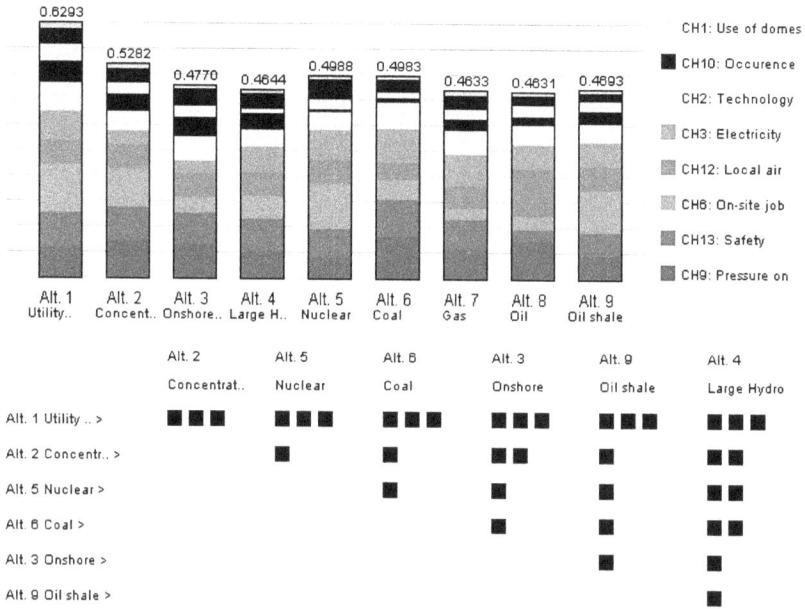

Figure 7.6 The final ranking of criteria from the Jordanian workshops.

emerged and all stakeholders could agree that the local solar power (utility PV) option was the best way to go. Thus, that became the recommendation for a national strategy in Jordan.

8

GUIDELINES FOR
REAL-LIFE DECISIONS

Now, we have almost reached the end of our journey through different decision models and ways of making decisions, focusing in particular on prescriptive real-world methods that are easily applicable. Hopefully, you have gained some understanding of how decisions could and should be made. This book is intended to be picked up whenever you have an important enough real-life decision to make, until the day you master the ideas and procedures well enough to perform them without guidance. To sum this book up, this short chapter will offer you some guidelines when picking your tools and procedures for making better decisions in the future. If the decision situation at hand is a smaller one, a more intuitive overall process can be followed. If it is larger, or a number of people or groups are involved, it is advisable to follow a more structured process as described in Chapters 4 and 6. In any case, the core of the process, intuitive or structured, is as follows.

As we stated at the beginning of Chapter 5, there are basically two development lines within decision theory in general as well as within prescriptive decision analysis – decisions made under a single criterion (with or without probabilities) and decisions involving several criteria. Let us consider them in turn.

8.1 Single-Criterion Decisions

Note the phrasing "made under a single criterion." This does not entail that there must be only one criterion, but, in many cases, one is so dominant that the others will only consume time to include either because of sheer dominance of one criterion in terms of importance, because the alternatives are fairly similar under the other conceivable criteria, or because the information for other criteria

DOI: 10.1201/9781003406709-8
99

is either unavailable or vague. In the ice cream parlour example in Chapters 2 and 3, the owner decided to focus only on net profit even though different, e.g., alternatives might influence the brand in different ways, thus making brand recognition a potential criterion, and alternatives might influence the possibility to rent the building in the long run. Both of the latter were too hard to estimate for the alternatives and were felt not to be influencing the decision enough if a clear best alternative was found. Only if the alternatives would have been close, those or other potential criteria might have warranted further investigation.

The first thing we do in the single criterion case is to collect the information we already have in the form of a P-C list. This contains our alternatives and their consequences. In Chapter 6 on the Pilot Method, this was described as Stage 1. While the Pilot Method is a method for multiple criteria, the P-C list compilation is done in the same way for a single criterion. The list is inspected for a clearly dominant alternative that renders further analysis unnecessary or for clearly inferior alternatives that can be purged from further processing.

Next, consider if we have a decision under strict uncertainty (Chapter 2) or under risk (Bayesian, Chapter 3). Again, it is not primarily a question of whether subjective probabilities exist. Rather, it is a question of whether it is worth the effort to include them in the model. They might be hard to estimate or they might be fairly equal, in both cases rendering them rather superfluous. If we have a strict uncertainty model, we use the decision rules from Chapter 2. Recall that Laplace's rule, taking the average, has the highest number of good properties and should be the first decision rule. If no clear alternative emerges as the winner from that, remove those that are obviously inferior and continue with Hurwicz' rule. For that rule, a parameter k should be chosen which expresses how to balance the highest and lowest outcomes among the alternatives. Most decision-makers have a decreasing utility curve and tend to view a lower worst outcome as more important to avoid than a lower best outcome. Thus, setting $k = 1/3$ is usually a good compromise for most decision-makers. If still no alternative emerges as the definitive best, the analysis should proceed as a decision under risk, i.e. probabilities should also be considered.

In decisions under risk, more than one possible outcome is considered and modelled for each alternative. We described this in Chapter 3 as a "two-party game." First, the decision-maker chooses one of the available alternatives, and thereafter, "nature chooses" which of the consequences will actually occur. Thus, the next task is to – for each outcome – estimate how likely it is to occur. In the paper-and-pen version, the one we saw in Chapter 3, the probabilities of a particular outcome are the same for all alternatives. Thus, in Table 3.1, we saw that, e.g., the probability for outcome S_1 is 0.25 (or 25%) for all three alternatives. In a risk decision matrix, for each alternative, the number in each column is multiplied by the probability on top of the column and then all these results are summed up to create the expected value. As discussed, the decision rule is to choose the alternative with the highest expected value (PMEV) after having performed a security level check. The latter entails a quite simple inspection of the matrix. First, consider which is the worst acceptable outcome (result) value that can be tolerated and call it s. Next, consider how probable such a result should be allowed to be and call that probability q. Then, visually scan each row (alternative), noting for each column if the column's value in this row is less than s, and if so, collect the column's probability. When all columns for an alternative have been scanned, sum up the collected probabilities, and if the sum exceeds q, then that alternative must be disregarded since it violates the security level that was set. A similar technique is used if no clear winner has emerged from the analysis after the security level and PMEV has been inspected. Remove all alternatives except those at the top according to PMEV that are indistinguishable since their expected values are rather equal. As a rule of thumb, "rather" means that they are within 5–10% of each other since the precision with which you assess the input information is seldom better than that (with the exception of tossing a fair coin and similar). The remaining alternatives are now scanned using a new threshold t (which is selected to be clearly above the security level), and the probabilities for the columns with values lower than t are again similarly summed up. The best alternative is the one with the lowest sum. Should the sums be rather equal, the procedure is repeated with a higher t until a winner emerges. If the decision situation contains a smaller set of alternatives and consequences, these methods are easily carried out using pen and paper. For larger sets, however, a spreadsheet is recommended – not because the calculations are complex but because it is easy to make a miscalculation or want to change some information in which case a spreadsheet does the recalculation in an instant once the model is in place. Lastly, if events are followed by other events (conditional probabilities), it is suggested to use a software program specifically designed for such more complex problems.

8.2 Multi-Criteria Decisions

For multi-criteria decision situations, we follow either the simpler Rank Three method from Chapter 5 or the more advanced Pilot Method described in Chapter 6. For a quick decision or when you might just want an illumination of the decision situation at hand, Rank Three is a very good method to employ. But for a more thorough decision analysis, though, the Pilot Method is recommended. A hallmark of that method is that it tries to keep the effort necessary for reaching a decision down. Thus, there is a possibility to conclude the process with a decision after any of the stages. In Stage 1, the situation is surveyed by putting the available information down in a P-C list per alternative (option). From that list, reasonable alternatives emerge together with their main advantages and disadvantages. Stage 2 is a refinement of the P-C lists in that the information that seems important enough is collected in clusters of similarity, thereby forming a first attempt at formulating the criteria. Usually, this stage brings a lot of clarity to the decision situation, and, in some cases, this is enough for making a decision. Often, though, the alternatives have their advantages and disadvantages in differing criteria and some kind of trade-off must be made. That is the topic of the remaining stages. Continuing with stage 3, after the criteria have been determined, the alternatives are ranked within each criterion. Completing that stage, we have a decision situation somewhat similar to the strict uncertainty case for a single-criterion decision in that we have information on the alternatives but not yet the way to sum them together (using probabilities for a single criterion, weights for multiple criteria). Akin to a single-criterion model, sometimes the information available is enough for making a decision, and if so, time and effort are saved.

Moving on to the last stages of the Pilot Method, a ranking of the criteria is introduced by which the model is in a sense complete and a decision can be made. For reasons of sensitivity analyses, there is also a step in Stage 4 which involves intuition in case the alternative that is pointed to as the best still does not convince the decision-maker. Multi-criteria decision situations are often complex, and it is important to make sure the result is transparent and well-understood. Akin to the single criterion case, if there is a small set of alternatives and criteria, pen and paper could easily be used. For larger decision situations, a spreadsheet is again recommended, and with a basic knowledge of spreadsheet modelling, it is no large effort to create such a model. Lastly, if the criteria are divided into sub-criteria in a criteria hierarchy, it is recommended to use a software program specifically designed for such more complex decision problems.

Can the above techniques be combined, i.e. is it possible to have events occurring for each alternative under each criterion in a multi-criteria decision situation? Yes, there is nothing in prescriptive decision theory that hinders or impedes the making or evaluation of such models. But they are excessively complex to calculate by hand, and even a spreadsheet soon becomes complicated. However, specialised software programs such as DecideIT, which is bundled with this book, have no problems building and evaluating those models.

Finally, there are two reminders. First, information in real-life situations is almost invariably a bit uncertain and you need to be prepared for that. One way, which could be a bit tedious for pen-and-paper calculations but is easy for spreadsheets, is to vary the numbers of the preferred alternative by small amounts and see if it sustains these changes, still coming out on top. Another, more direct way is to require the best alternative to surpass the others with a reasonable margin, where "reasonable" is context-dependent but often in the range of 5–10% above the second-rated alternative, especially if monetary values are being used.

Second, intuition is good as a companion when making decisions but not as a pilot. Thus, intuition should be used as a checkpoint late in or after the analysis. If the selected best alternative does not feel intuitively reasonable, then either some assumption is wrong, leading to the wrong result, or the intuition points in the wrong direction. Because of the transparency of prescriptive methods, the unintuitive result can be traced back to its roots to find either some erroneous fact or parameter or a misunderstanding of some information. Either way, such an intuition checkpoint usually leads to an even better understanding of both the input information and the ensuing decision to make.

Having said that, we have now reached the end of the book and hope that we have provided you with a number of valuable and effective decision methods for a variety of decision situations and wish you the best of luck in applying them and making good decisions with the help of them.

Appendix:

The DecideIT Software

A licence for the decision-supporting and decision-analytical software program DecideIT is included with this book. The program is a user-friendly tool developed for MS Windows by Preference AB and has been used in some of the examples in this book. It can handle various aspects of decisions with multiple criteria as well as event trees (probabilities). There is no need to enter precise information in order to be able to receive adequate decision support. Instead, rather vague information can be used but still be sufficient in order to find out which decision alternative is the preferred one, given available data. The decision software DecideIT has several properties and features as follows:

- A good overview to obtain a better overall picture
- Easy to document, review, and adjust the underlying data
- Hard problems are solvable within a reasonable time
- Supports imprecise probabilities, consequence values, and criteria weights
- Supports rankings of values, weights, and probabilities instead of, or combined with, numerical data
- Supports evaluation of combined multi-criteria and event probability decision problems
- Simple ways of detecting a lack of information

In real-life problems, it is usually impossible to assign precise numerical values to the different components of a decision, and there is hence a need for representation and evaluation mechanisms that can handle (sometimes severe) incompleteness of information.

DecideIT allows the construction of models that are actually useful in real-life practice, in that they allow decision-makers to only provide imprecise information but still gain important insights into the decision problems at hand. This is in contrast to either decision-making using artificially precise input or decision-making based on diffuse gut feelings and impulses.

For this short introduction to the tool, the decision example consists of whether a new information system should be acquired and implemented by a company. This simplified situation contains only three alternatives – making an investment in one of two vendors' systems or making no investment.

To start a session, first launch DecideIT. Double-click on DecideIT in the program menu or on your desktop.

To begin modelling, click the New symbol in the toolbar. (In the File menu, you can also create a New model. Further, you can Open an existing one, Close or Save a current model, and Exit the program. But most menu commands also have easy-access symbols in the toolbar, and if so, we will refer to those in the first place.)

A pop-up dialogue will appear, in which you can select the model type and the number of alternatives (called strategies in the program) (see Figure A.1). In this example, we will use a multi-criteria model of the kind we saw in Chapters 5–7.

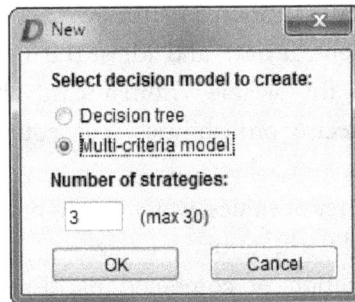

Figure A.1   Selecting a multi-criteria model.

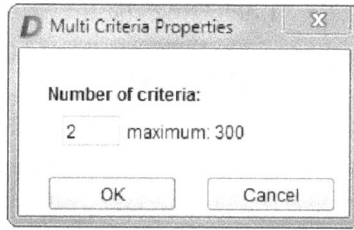

Figure A.2 Selecting number of criteria.

The default number of alternatives is two, but we will have three in the example. Enter the number of alternatives and click OK. In the next pop-up window, the number of criteria for this multi-criteria decision situation is entered (see Figure A.2). To keep this example simple, we stay with the default of two criteria while the program is able to handle up to 300. Both the number of criteria and the number of alternatives (henceforth called "strategies" to comply with the program terminology) are possible to change later while working with the program. The numbers entered now are only for the initial model.

Click OK to have an initial model created. The program now enters its basic mode with access to all open models. There can be as many as 50 open models, but we will only have 1 open in this appendix.

Each open model resides in a separate window (see Figure A.3). On top of all windows are the menu bar and the toolbar. Several of the items in the toolbar are grey at any given moment when running the program. This only shows that not all functions are applicable at all times and with all models. In our example, we face a decision of investing in a new information system for customer service. The old one is increasingly inappropriate, given the new market demands and expansion plans of our business, but it could still work for a couple of years. The choice is between system vendors A and B, with the

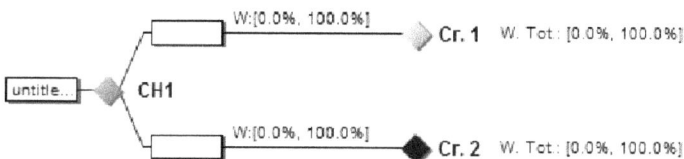

Figure A.3 Multi-criteria model with two criteria.

additional third strategy of deferring the investment for a few years, to the end of the projected possible lifetime of the current system. Reasons for deferring the investment include the strategy and market outlook of the business as well as the expected development plans of the system vendors. On the other hand, important market shares might be lost if and when the market takes off in the near future.

The decision model is initially constructed in three steps. It is important to follow the steps in order. The steps are as follows:

1. Identify and name the criteria and the alternatives
2. Enter value estimates for each alternative under each criterion
3. Enter importance estimates for each criterion

A.1 Step 1 – Identify and Name the Criteria and the Alternatives

In this simplified example, we will use only two criteria: cost and performance. Let us enter these label names into DecideIT by right-clicking on the respective criteria. Then, a dialogue box will appear where you can enter the criterion name. Click OK and enter the other criterion name in the same manner. Further, you can name the decision problem in a similar way by right-clicking on the leftmost rectangle. Then, your model will look like this. If you like to have the labels spelt out in full, you can enlarge the rectangles in the menu option Tools > Settings, where you can enter a larger pixel width for the rectangles in the form of a number or by pulling the handle. Step 1 is now almost finished. The only sub-step that remains is giving names to the strategies. Select the S symbol on the toolbar. In the dialogue box, enter the names by clicking Rename. As you can see, here you can edit the number of strategies (alternatives), should that become required in a later phase of the analysis. This concludes Step 1.

A.2 Step 2 – Enter Information about the Strategies (Alternatives)

The values of each alternative under each criterion can be entered in two ways: either as (imprecise) numbers or as rankings, the latter in case you have a criterion where it is hard to give numbers. This could be a criterion such as business image, but both our criteria are reasonably quantifiable. Assume that the costs for each alternative have been estimated as follows for the next three years of operation:

- *System vendor A*: Between 2.9 and 4.2 MEUR
- *System vendor B*: Between 3.7 and 5.5 MEUR
- *No investment*: Between 0.6 and 1.1 MEUR

The strategy not to invest still incurs licence and maintenance costs.

To enter the costs in DecideIT, right-click on the Cost criterion. In the dialogue box, select the tab Values/Connection (see Figure A.4). In this tab, the cost of each strategy can be entered as a fixed number (seldom used), an interval, or an interval with a most likely number. In our case, we have intervals and thus select Option 2 for the radio buttons on the left. Note that higher costs are less preferred; thus, the costs should be entered as negative numbers. The ranges of the intervals express the degree of uncertainty of each statement.

Further assume that the performance is a combined measure of the number of customers, revenue per customer, and customer satisfaction. In a real-life case, these would be separate criteria, but to keep this example manageable, they have been concatenated. Assume that this combined measure yields the following estimates:

- *System vendor A*: Between 45 and 75
- *System vendor B*: Between 55 and 90
- *No investment*: Between 10 and 35

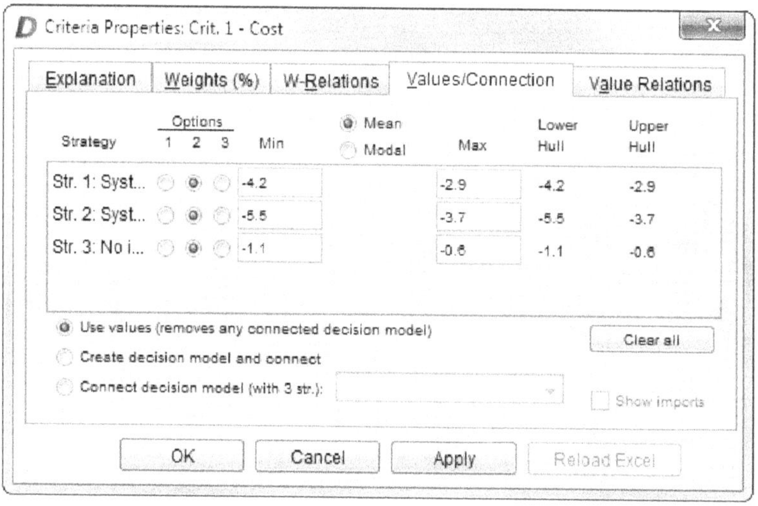

Figure A.4 Costs entered as negative values.

They are entered in the same manner by right-clicking on the Performance rectangle and then selecting the Values/Connection tab. Click OK. This concludes Step 2 of the data entry.

A.3 Step 3 – Determine the Importance of the Criteria

We have two criteria and their relative importance should be input next. It should be noted that it is the difference in importance between the criteria in this decision problem that should be compared. For example, if the difference in cost between the alternatives is small, then the criterion cost is ranked low *for this particular case*. This does not say anything about the general view on cost within a business – which often is at the top of management's attention. Thus, the range of possible numbers for each criterion is what should be compared. To view these so-called scale spans, select Set Value Scale from the Edit menu to obtain a pop-up window (see Figure A.5). In this window, we can see that cost ranges between 0.6 and 5.5 MEUR while performance ranges between 10 and 90 points. Thus, the cost range [−5.5, −0.6] should importance-wise be compared to the performance range [10, 90].

Given these value scales, the team of decision-makers finds that the difference in performance between the best and the worst outcome is more important than the difference in cost between the best

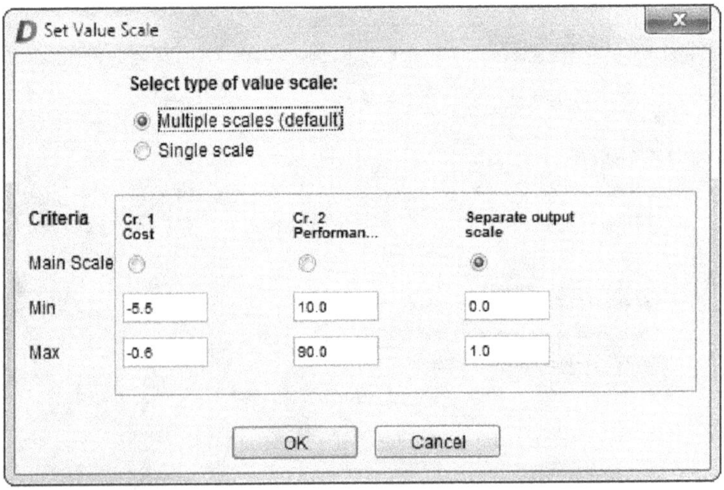

Figure A.5   Multiple scales with different endpoints.

Figure A.6 Criteria weights as percentages.

and the worst outcome. They assign the following weights to the respective criteria:

- *Cost*: 35%–45%
- *Performance*: 55%–65%

Note that, in the same manner as for values, by right-clicking on a criterion and selecting the Weights tab, the weights can be entered as fixed numbers (although it is unusual to know weights with full precision), as intervals, or as intervals with an additional most likely percentage (see Figure A.6). The widths of the intervals express the degree of uncertainty in each statement.

These statements of importance of the criteria are all we need to evaluate the decision situation. After the three data entry steps, the next step is to evaluate the decision situation.

A.4 Step 4 – Evaluation

To start evaluating, begin with the main evaluation window. It is reached by selecting General Overview in the Evaluation menu. Then the following evaluation result window will appear (see Figure A.7).

In this window, you can see in the upper half that strategy 2, investing in a system from vendor B, is the preferred strategy (alternative of action). The heights of the bars represent how preferred they

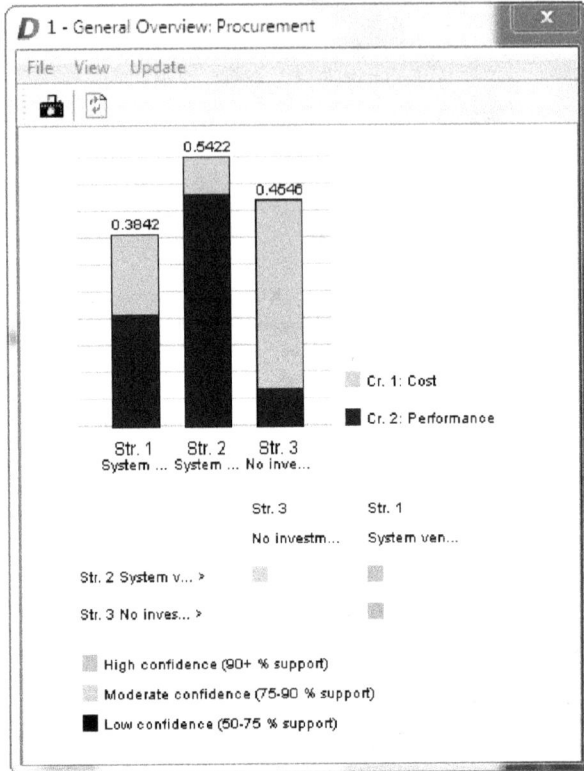

Figure A.7   Results of the evaluation.

are, with the numbers on top of the bars indicating the percentage of fulfilment compared to a fictitious optimal alternative. Such choices seldom exist in reality, e.g., the best performance for the lowest cost (and if they do, they are most often easily identifiable without any decision analysis tool). In the lower half of the window, there are comparisons on how much confidence can be put into one strategy being ranked higher than another. We can see that Strategy 1 (Vendor A) is dominated with high confidence while Vendor B wins over no investment with moderate confidence. In this example, the result is due to there only being two criteria. A larger set of criteria is usually more discriminative when it comes to confidence levels.

Next, you can gain an overview of where the confidence in the belief in the different strategies is allocated. To find that out, consult the pie chart by clicking on that symbol in the toolbar or selecting

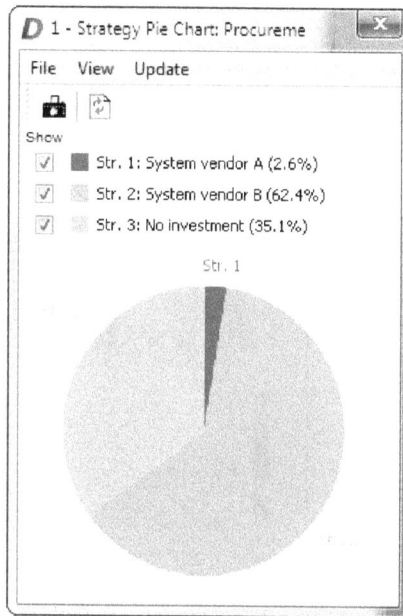

Figure A.8   Pie chart showing belief in alternatives.

Evaluation > Pie Chart in the menu. Then, the following pie chart appears (see Figure A.8).

From it, you can tell that Strategy 1 is lagging far behind and can reasonably be excluded from further analyses unless new, more favourable information arrives. Around two-thirds of the belief rests on Strategy 2 and the rest on the non-investment strategy.

Next, you can investigate the overlap in results for the three strategies. By clicking on the vertical bars in the toolbar or selecting Evaluation > Bar Chart, a dialogue pop-up appears in which you can choose at which confidence (support) level you want to investigate the possible resulting ranges for the strategies (see Figure A.9). Since 90% is a reasonable support level, you can keep that default suggestion and click OK. Now you can see what you have already been shown, just presented in a complementary way – this time as resulting values relative to each other, i.e. 0 means being equally good as the average of all strategies. As opposed to the two previous ways of displaying the results, this one will be affected if an inferior strategy is removed. For that reason, this function is presented as the third way of illustrating the evaluation results.

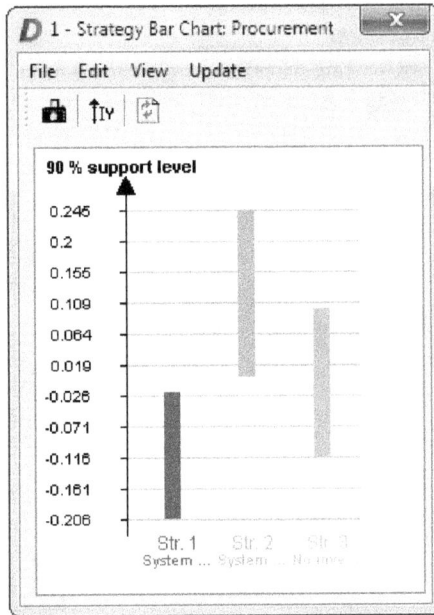

Figure A.9   Bar chart showing overlap in outcomes.

Again, Strategy 1 is clearly inferior. If a decision is imminent, Strategy 2 is the most preferred one. But in a real-life case with some more time remaining, it is important to go back and revalidate the input information.

Note that this example does not in any sense purport to be realistic in its input values or number of criteria or alternatives. It was conceived only to demonstrate DecideIT in the easiest possible way. On the contrary, a more realistic case has more alternative values under maybe five to ten criteria or more. It is when the situation becomes more complex that software programs such as DecideIT show their strengths by showing results that the human mind is not possible to compute.

A.5 Installation

How to install DecideIT on a Microsoft Windows PC (from Windows 7 and upwards):

1. Download the program from the Preference website www. preference.nu/digitrans.
2. Follow the installation instructions to install the program.

3. Once installed, click on the DecideIT icon on your desktop or program menu to start the program for the first time.
4. The program will ask for the licence key, a procedure which is explained below.
5. For all consecutive starts, up until the expiry of the licence, all functionality will be as above in the guide.

A.6 Licence Key Entry

With this book comes a one-year single-user licence for DecideIT. This licence is valid for one user and for one year after its entry into the program, after which you can continue to use the program in demo mode or purchase a renewal of the licence.

The right to use the licence is granted only to the original acquirer of the book and cannot be transferred by trading the book.

The first time you start the program, you are prompted for a licence key. You should enter the key (as supplied in this book or if you bought an additional licence) into the key subfields. Once the licence key is entered, the expiry date of its active use is determined by the program and you are good to go for one year.

> **DecideIT licence key**
>
> **971F-B82-06B-1B8-FCF**

The appendix and licence key are courtesy of Preference AB, the company that manufactures and sells this product.

Reading Tips

This is a list of fundamental books for the interested reader who wants to gain a deeper understanding of the mechanisms behind decision-making. Although none of the books (except our own) directly address the prescriptive perspective, they are nevertheless good reads even though most of them are at a considerably more advanced level than this book you are currently reading.

R. T. Clemen, *Making Hard Decisions*, Brooks/Cole Publishing Co., Pacific Grove, CA, 1996.

L. Ekenberg, K. Hansson, M. Danielson, and G. Cars, *Deliberation, Representation, Equity*, Open Book Publishers, Cambridge, UK, 2017.

S. French, *Decision Theory – An Introduction to the Mathematics of Rationality*, Ellis Horwood Ltd., Hempstead Herts, UK, 1988.

D. Kahneman, *Thinking, Fast and Slow*, Penguin Books, London, UK, 2011.

R. L. Keeney, *Value-Focused Thinking – A Path to Creative Decisionmaking*, Harvard University Press, Cambridge, MA, 1992.

R. L. Keeney and H. Raiffa, *Decisions with Multiple Objectives – Preferences and Value Tradeoffs*, Wiley, New York, NY, 1976.

R. D. Luce and H. Raiffa, *Games and Decisions – Introduction and Critical Survey*, John Wiley and Sons, New York, NY, 1957.

M. G. Morgan and M. Henrion, *Uncertainty: A Guide to Dealing with Uncertainty in Quantitative Risk and Policy Analysis*, Cambridge University Press, Cambridge, MA, 1990.

H. Raiffa, *Decision Analysis: Introductory Lectures and Choices under Uncertainty*, Random House, New York, NY, 1968.

M. D. Resnik, *Choices – An Introduction to Decision Theory*, University of Minnesota Press, Minneapolis, MN, 1987.

T. L. Saaty, *The Analytical Hierarchy Process*, McGraw Hill, New York, NY, 1980.

L. J. Savage, *The Foundation of Statistics*, Dover Publications, New York, NY, 1972.

H. Simon, *Models of Thought*, Yale University Press, New Haven, CN, 1979.

P. Vincke, *Multicriteria Decision Aid*, John Wiley and Sons, Chichester, UK, 1992.

P. Walley, *Statistical Reasoning with Imprecise Probabilities*, Chapman and Hall, London, UK, 1991.

K. Weichselberger and S. Pöhlmann, *A Methodology for Uncertainty in Knowledge-Based Systems*, Springer-Verlag, New York, NY, 1990.

References

M. Allais, The Foundations of a Positive Theory of Choice involving Risk and a Criticism of the Postulates and Axioms of the American School (originally in French 1953), in M. Allais. and O. Hagen (eds.), *Expected Utility Hypotheses and the Allais Paradox*. D. Reidel Publishing Company, Dordrecht, the Netherlands, 1979.

F. H. Barron and B. E. Barrett, Decision quality using ranked attribute weights, *Management Science* 42(11), 1515–1523, 1996.

T. Bayes, An essay toward solving a problem in the doctrine of chances, *Philosophical Transactions of the Royal Society of London* 53, 370–418, 1763.

D. Bernoulli, *Specimen Theoriae Novae de Mensura Sortis*, translated in English into Theory on the Measurement of Risk, Econometrica 22, pp. 22–36, 1954 (original from 1738).

G. Cardano, *Liber de ludo aleae (Book on games of chance)*, in Latin 1663. Reprinted by Princeton University Press, Princeton, NJ, 1953.

A. de Moivre, *Miscellanea Analytica*, Tonson & Watts, London, UK, 1730.

A. de Moivre, *The Doctrine of Chances* (2nd ed.), Woodfall, London, UK, 1738. Reprinted by Cass, London, UK, 1967.

A. P. Dempster, Upper and lower probabilities induced by a multivalued mapping, *Annals of Mathematical Statistics* 38, 325–339, 1967.

W. Edwards, Social utilities, *Engineering Economist*, Summer Symposium Series 6, 119–129, 1971.

D. Ellsberg, Risk, ambiguity, and the Savage axioms, *Quarterly Journal of Economics* 75, 643–669, 1961.

L. Fibonacci, *Liber Abaci (Book of calculation)*, Latin manuscript, 1202. Reprinted as B. Boncompagni (Ed.), Scritti di Leonardo Pisano, Vol.1, Tipografia della scienze matematiche e fisiche, Rome, Italy, 1857.

P. C. Fishburn, Transitive measurable utility, *Journal of Economic Theory* 31, 293–317, 1983.

S. French, *Decision Theory – An Introduction to the Mathematics of Rationality*, Ellis Horwood, Chichester, West Sussex, UK, 1988.

P. Gärdenfors and N.-E. Sahlin, Unreliable probabilities, risk taking, and decision making, *Synthese* 53, 361–386, 1982.

L. Hurwicz, Optimality Criteria for Decision Making under Ignorance, Cowles Commission Discussion Paper No. 370, 1951.

D. Kahneman, *Thinking, Fast and Slow*, Penguin Books, London, UK, 2011.

R. L. Keeney, Decision analysis: an overview, *Operations Research*, 30, 803–838, 1982.

R. L. Keeney and H. Raiffa, *Decisions with Multiple Objectives: Preferences and Value Trade-offs*, John Wiley & Sons, New York, NY, 1976.

J. M. Keynes, *A Treatise on Probability*, McMillan and Co, London, UK, 1921.

J. M. Keynes, The general theory of employment, *The Quarterly Journal of Economics* 51, 212–223, 1937.

A. N. Kolmogorov, *Grundbegriffe der Wahrscheinlichkeitsrechnung*, Springer Verlag, Berlin, Germany, 1933.

A. N. Kolmogorov, On the analytic methods of probability theory, *Uspekhi Matematicheskikh Nauk* 5, 5–41, 1938.

P-S. Laplace, *Théorie Analytique des Probabilités*, Courcier, Paris, 1812.

P-S. Laplace, *Essai Philosophique sur les Probabilites*, 3rd ed., Courcier, Paris, 1816. (Translation published by Dover 1952.)

G. Loomes and R. Sugden, Regret theory: an alternative theory of rational choice under uncertainty, *The Economic Journal* 92, 805–924, 1982.

R. D. Luce and H. Raiffa, *Games and Decisions – Introduction and Critical Survey*, John Wiley & Sons, New York, NY, 1957.

P.-E. Malmnäs, Evaluations, Preferences, and Choice Rules, Internal report, Department of Philosophy, Stockholm University, 1996.

B. Mareschal, J.-P. Brans, and P. Vincke, Prométhée: A New Family of Outranking Methods in Multicriteria Analysis, in J.-P. Brans (ed.), *Operational Research 1984 International Conference Proceedings*, pp. 477–490, North Holland/Elsevier Science, Amsterdam, The Netherlands, 1984.

K. Menger, Das Unsicherheitsmoment in der Wertlehre. *Zeitschrift für Nationalökonomie* 5, 459–485, 1934.

J. Milnor, Games against Nature, in R.M. Thrall, C.H. Coombs, and R.L. Davis (eds.), *Decision Processes*, pp. 49–59, John Wiley & Sons, New York, NY, 1954.

P.-R. Montmort (1678–1719), *Essay d'Analyse sur les Jeux de Hazard*, Le Conte, Paris, France, 1708.

M. G. Morgan and M. Henrion, *Uncertainty: A Guide to Dealing with Uncertainty in Quantitative Risk and Policy Analyses*, Cambridge University Press, Cambridge, MA, 1990.

L. Paccioli, *Summa de arithmetica, geometria et proportionalità*, Compendium, 615 pages, Venice, Italy, 1494.

J. Quiggin, A theory of anticipated utility, *Journal of Economic Behavior and Organisation* 3, 323–343, 1982.

F. P. Ramsey, Truth and Probability (essay from 1926), in R.B. Braithwaite (ed.), *The Foundations of Mathematics and other Logical Essays*, Ch. VII, pp. 156–198, Kegan, Paul, Trench, Trubner & Co., London, UK, 1931.

M. D. Resnik, *Choices – An Introduction to Decision Theory*, University of Minnesota Press, Minneapolis, MN, 1987.

B. Roy, The outranking approach and the foundations of the ELECTRE methods, *Theory and Decision* 31, 49–73, 1991.

T. L. Saaty, Scaling method for priorities in hierarchical structures, *Journal of Mathematical Psychology* 15(3), 234–281, 1977.

L. J. Savage, The theory of statistical decision, *Journal of the American Statistical Association* 46(253), 55–67, 1951.

L. J. Savage, *The Foundation of Statistics*, 2nd ed., Dover Publications, New York, NY, 1972. (First edition 1954).

G. Shafer, *A Mathematical Theory of Evidence*, Princeton University Press, Princeton, NJ, 1976.

P. Slovic and A. Tversky, Who accepts Savage's axiom? *Systems Research and Behavioral Science* 19, 368–373, 1974.

W. G. Stillwell, D. A. Seaver, and W. Edwards, A comparison of weight approximation techniques in multiattribute utility decision making, *Organizational Behavior and Human Performance* 28(1), 62–77, 1981.

R. von Mises, *Probability, Statistics and Truth*, George Allen and Unwin, London, UK, 1928.

J. von Neumann, Zur Theorie der Gesellschaftsspiele, *Mathematische Annalen* 100, 295–320, 1928.

J. von Neumann and O. Morgenstern, *Theory of Games and Economic Behaviour*, Princeton University Press, Princeton, NJ, 1944. (second edition 1947).

A. Wald, *Statistical Decision Functions*, John Wiley & Sons, New York, NY, 1950.

P. Walley, *Statistical Reasoning with Imprecise Probabilities*, Chapman and Hall, London, UK, 1991.

P. Walley, Imprecise Probabilities, The Imprecise Probabilities Project, available at https://web.archive.org/web/19991010012219/http://ensmain. rug.ac.be/~ipp/documentation/introduction/introduction.html, 1997. Accessed 2023-05-01.

K. Weichselberger, The theory of interval-probability as a unifying concept for uncertainty, *International Journal of Approximate Reasoning* 24(2–3), 149–170, 1999.

K. Weichselberger and S. Pöhlmann, *A Methodology for Uncertainty in Knowledge-Based Systems*, Springer-Verlag, New York, NY, 1990.

M. Yaari, The dual theory of choice under risk, *Econometrica* 55, 95–115, 1987.

L. A. Zadeh, Fuzzy sets, *Information and Control* 8(3), 338–353, 1965.

Index

A

Additive value rule, 54
Admissible alternative, 7, 44
Allais, M., x, 30
Allais' paradox, 30–31, 33
Analysis of argumentation, 14
Analytic Hierarchy Process (AHP), 57
Argument Matrix, 68–69, 72
Arrow, K., x
Artificial intelligence, 8, 38
Availability cascades, 32, 43
Axiom system, 8–9, 28

B

Bandwagon effects, 32, 43
Barrett, B.E., 58
Barron, F.H., 58
Base rate fallacy, 32, 43
Bayes, T., 4
Bayes' theorem, 4
Bayesian decisions, 7, 21–34, 37, 53–54, 100

Bernoulli, D., 4–5, 27
Bounded rationality, 9, 32–33
Brans, J-P., 58

C

Cardano, G., 3
Chance nodes, 23, 26
Column duplication, 19
Complete ranking, 18
Conditional probability, 21–22, 26, 102
Consequence nodes, 23, 26
Constant independence, 19
Cost analysis, 79
Course of action, 3, 12–13, 21, 40, 43, 46, 51
Cramer, G., 27
Criteria trade-off, x, 53, 56, 64, 90, 102

D

DecideIT, 48, 63, 103, 105–115
Decision nodes, 23, 26

Decision process, 11, 21, 40–45, 63–83
Decision rule, 2, 5, 7, 9, 11, 14–19, 21–29, 43–44, 100–101
Decision table, 13–18, 61
Decision theory, 22, 26, 29–32, 43, 53, 99, 103
Decision tree, 23, 26, 40, 50
Decisions under certainty, 13–14
Decisions under risk, 13, 21–34
Decisions under strict uncertainty, 11, 13–19
Dempster, A.P., 38–39
Deontic decision rules, 2
Descartes, R., 2–3
Descriptive decision theory, xi, 9, 32, 43
Direct rating, 54–55

E

Edwards, W., 55, 58
ELECTRE, 58
Ellsberg's paradox, 30–31
Energy planning (example), 93–97
Event nodes, 23
Exaggerated expectations, 32, 43
Exclusive consequence set, 12–13, 42, 46
Exhaustive consequence set, 12, 22, 42, 46
Expected loss, 7
Expected utility, 5, 7, 9, 21–22, 29, 31
Expected value, 5, 19, 25–26, 29, 32–33, 43–44, 49–50, 54, 101

F

de Fermat, P., 3
Fibonacci, 3
Fight-flight-fright response, 1

Fishburn, P.C., 33
Folding back, 26
Føllesdal, D., 29
Forward analysis, 83–84
Framing, 3, 32, 43
French, S., 8
Fuzzy set theory, 38–39

G

Gambling, 3, 28–29
Game theory, 7, 11, 15
Gärdenfors, P., 37
Gombaud, A. 3
Group thinking, 32

H

Henrion, M., 35
Hurwicz, L., x, 15, 18, 100

I

Imprecise information, 35–53
Information cascades, 32, 43
Insurance, 3, 34, 43
Interval decision analysis, 35–53
Inverse analysis, 83
Irrelevance independence, 19

K

Kahneman, D., x–xi, 9
Keeney, R., 8, 53
Keynes, J.M., 6
Kleinmuntz, D., 74
Kolmogorov, A.N., 31, 38

L

Laplace, P-S., 4, 14–15, 19, 24, 100
Loomes, G., 33
Luce, R.D., 13

M

Malmnäs, P-E., 33
Mareschal, B., 58
Markowitz, H., 9
Maximax principle, 16–18
Maximin principle, 14–18
Menger, K., 27–28
Milnor, J., 14–19
Minimax-regret principle, 15–16
von Mises, R., 6
de Moivre, A., 4
Montmort, P-R., 3
Morgan, M.G., 35
Morgenstern, O., 7, 28

N

Nature, 6, 11, 23–24, 101
Nobel Prize, x
Normalisation, 54–55
Normative decision theory, x–xi, 9,
        28, 32, 34
von Neumann, J., 7, 28

O

Objective probability, 6–7, 11, 24,
        31, 35

P

Paccioli, L., 3
Pascal, B., 3
Pen-and-paper methods, 58,
        103
Pessimism-optimism index, 15
Pilot Method, 14, 57–59, 63–84,
        87, 100, 102–103
PMEV, 26–34, 43–44, 101
Pöhlmann, S., 38
Point allocation, 54–56
Policy formation (example), 89–93

Prescriptive decision theory, xi,
        9–10, 28, 31–34, 99, 103
Principle of insufficient reason,
        14–15
Pro-and-contra list (P-C list),
        64–71, 100–102
Procurement (example), 65, 85–89
PROMETHEE, 58
Proportional scoring, 55–57

Q

Quiggin, J., 33

R

Raiffa, H., 13, 23, 53
Ramsey, F.P., 6–7, 28
Rank order centroid (ROC), 58
Rank reciprocal weights, 58
Rank sum weights, 58
Rank Three, 59–62, 102
Ratio scoring, 57
Rationality, ix, 3, 6–10, 14, 18, 21,
        24, 28–29, 32–34
Resnik, M.D., 8
Risk matrix, 25
Risk neutrality, 26, 29
Risk-free (deterministic) world, 2, 13
Rolling back tree, 26
Row permutation independence, 19

S

Saaty, T.L., 57
Sahlin, N-E., 37
Sample space, 22
Sanity checks, 41, 43
Savage, L.J., 7, 15–16, 30
Seaver, D.A., 58
Security levels, 34, 43, 49, 67, 101
Shafer, G., 38–39
Simon, H., x, 9

Simos, J., 58–59
Slovic, P., 32
SMART, 55–57
St. Petersburg Paradox, 4–5, 27
Stillwell, W.G., 58
Stirling, J., 4
Strict uncertainty, 11–19, 100–102
Strong domination, 18
Subjective probability, 4–6, 11, 21– 35
Sure-thing principle, 27, 30
Surrogate weights, 57–59, 88

T

Teleological decision rules, 2
Temporal decision order, 24
Tree pruning, 26
Tversky, A., 9, 32

U

Uncertain reasoning, 8
Utility theory, x, 7, 9, 26, 28, 30, 36, 39

V

Value scale independence, 18
Vincke. P., 58

W

Wald, A., 7, 14–17
Walley, P., 36–38
Weichselberger, K., 38
Weight/scale duality, 56

Y

Yaari, M., 33

Z

Zadeh, L.A., 38

For Product Safety Concerns and Information please contact our EU
representative GPSR@taylorandfrancis.com
Taylor & Francis Verlag GmbH, Kaufingerstraße 24, 80331 München, Germany